CAMBRIDGE LIBRARY COLLECTION

Books of enduring scholarly value

Linguistics

From the earliest surviving glossaries and translations to nineteenth-century academic philology and the growth of linguistics during the twentieth century, language has been the subject both of scholarly investigation and of practical handbooks produced for the upwardly mobile, as well as for travellers, traders, soldiers, missionaries and explorers. This collection will reissue a wide range of texts pertaining to language, including the work of Latin grammarians, groundbreaking early publications in Indo-European studies, accounts of indigenous languages, many of them now extinct, and texts by pioneering figures such as Jacob Grimm, Wilhelm von Humboldt and Ferdinand de Saussure.

Two Representative Tribes of Queensland

John Mathew was a Presbyterian minister who developed an interest in Aboriginal ethnography after migrating from Scotland to work on his uncle's farm in Queensland in 1864. From 1879 he published influential studies of Aboriginal culture. Although Mathew's speculative argument for the tri-hybrid origins of the Australian Aborigines has long been disproved, his discussion of Aboriginal language and social behaviour was pioneering in the field of anthropology and is still well-regarded today. *Two Representative Tribes of Queensland* (1910) is the result of extensive time Mathew spent visiting the Kabi and Wakka people living in the Barambah Government Aboriginal Station. This direct experience is emphasised in the preface to the book: 'For Mr Mathew Australian origins ... have been a life study, and the knowledge bearing upon these questions, which most others have gleaned from the library shelves, he has acquired at first-hand in the native camping grounds.'

T0370840

Cambridge University Press has long been a pioneer in the reissuing of out-of-print titles from its own backlist, producing digital reprints of books that are still sought after by scholars and students but could not be reprinted economically using traditional technology. The Cambridge Library Collection extends this activity to a wider range of books which are still of importance to researchers and professionals, either for the source material they contain, or as landmarks in the history of their academic discipline.

Drawing from the world-renowned collections in the Cambridge University Library, and guided by the advice of experts in each subject area, Cambridge University Press is using state-of-the-art scanning machines in its own Printing House to capture the content of each book selected for inclusion. The files are processed to give a consistently clear, crisp image, and the books finished to the high quality standard for which the Press is recognised around the world. The latest print-on-demand technology ensures that the books will remain available indefinitely, and that orders for single or multiple copies can quickly be supplied.

The Cambridge Library Collection will bring back to life books of enduring scholarly value (including out-of-copyright works originally issued by other publishers) across a wide range of disciplines in the humanities and social sciences and in science and technology.

Two Representative Tribes of Queensland

*With an Inquiry Concerning
the Origin of the Australian Race*

JOHN MATHEW
A. KEANE

CAMBRIDGE
UNIVERSITY PRESS

CAMBRIDGE UNIVERSITY PRESS

Cambridge, New York, Melbourne, Madrid, Cape Town, Singapore,
São Paolo, Delhi, Dubai, Tokyo

Published in the United States of America by Cambridge University Press, New York

www.cambridge.org
Information on this title: www.cambridge.org/9781108009287

This edition first published 1910
This digitally printed version 2010

ISBN 978-1-108-00928-7 Paperback

TWO REPRESENTATIVE TRIBES OF QUEENSLAND

TWO REPRESENTATIVE TRIBES OF QUEENSLAND

WITH AN INQUIRY CONCERNING THE ORIGIN OF THE AUSTRALIAN RACE

BY

JOHN MATHEW, M.A., B.D.

AUTHOR OF "EAGLEHAWK AND CROW," "AUSTRALIAN ECHOES," ETC.

WITH AN INTRODUCTION BY

PROF. A. H. KEANE, LL.D., F.R.A.I., F.R.G.S.

LATE VICE-PRESIDENT R. ANTHROP. INSTITUTE

AUTHOR OF "ETHNOLOGY," "MAN PAST AND PRESENT," "THE WORLD'S PEOPLES," ETC.

AND A MAP AND SIX ILLUSTRATIONS

T. FISHER UNWIN

LONDON
ADELPHI TERRACE

LEIPSIC
INSELSTRASSE 20

1910

DEDICATED TO

J. H. MACFARLAND, Esq., M.A., LL.D.,

MASTER OF ORMOND COLLEGE,
VICE-CHANCELLOR OF MELBOURNE UNIVERSITY,
AND A MEMBER OF THE BOARD FOR THE PROTECTION OF THE
ABORIGINES IN THE STATE OF VICTORIA,
AS A MARK OF ESTEEM
AND A TOKEN OF APPRECIATION OF HIS SERVICES
TO THE CAUSE OF LEARNING.

CONTENTS

CHAP.   PAGE

          INTRODUCTION - - - - xi

          PREFACE - - - - - xxi

    I. INQUIRY CONCERNING THE ORIGIN OF THE AUSTRALIAN RACE - - - 25

    II. THE COUNTRY OF THE KABI AND WAKKA TRIBES - - - - - 67

    III. PHYSICAL AND MENTAL CHARACTERS - 72

    IV. DAILY LIFE—SHELTER—FOOD—CLOTHING - 83

    V. MAN-MAKING AND OTHER CEREMONIES - 97

    VI. DISEASE AND TREATMENT—DEATH—BURIAL AND MOURNING - - 110

    VII. ART — IMPLEMENTS — UTENSILS —WEAPONS —CORROBOREES - - - 117

    VIII. SOCIAL ORGANISATION - - - 128

    IX. THE FAMILY—KINSHIP AND MARRIAGE - 153

    X. RELIGION AND MAGIC - - - 167

    XI. MYTHS AND LEGENDS - - - 179

    XII. LANGUAGE - - - - - 198

          VOCABULARY - - - - - 225

LIST OF ILLUSTRATIONS

MAP OF COUNTRY OF THE KABI AND WAKKA
    TRIBES -   -   -   - *Facing p.* 67

TOMMY CAIN OF YABBER, MARY RIVER,
    QUEENSLAND -   -   -   -   ,,   74

TURANDIU, SON OF DICK AND FANNY   -   ,,   75

A NATIVE OF THE KABI TRIBE, MARY-
    BOROUGH, QUEENSLAND   -   ,,   121

NATIVES OF YABBER, KABI TRIBE, MARY
    RIVER, QUEENSLAND -   -   -   ,,   124

KAGARIU, OR JOHNNIE CAMPBELL, OF KABI
    TRIBE, MARY RIVER, QUEENSLAND,
    THE MOST NOTORIOUS NATIVE BUSH-
    RANGER -   -   -   -   -   ,,   137

A COMPARATIVELY STRAIGHT-HAIRED AND A
    CURLY - HAIRED MAN, NATIVES OF
    YABBER, KABI TRIBE, MARY RIVER,
    QUEENSLAND   -   -   ,,   138

INTRODUCTION

It is with peculiar pleasure that I have responded to the author's invitation to supply a few preliminary remarks to this solid and well-reasoned essay on Austro-Tasmanian origins. Apart from its general interest, the subject is one which has always had a special fascination for me, and I the more readily avail myself of this opportunity to say a few words on some of its more obscure problems inasmuch as I am substantially in accord with the views here advanced by Mr Mathew. We both hold that the Australians are a hybrid race, whose basal element is the Papuasian, but represented in recent times by the now extinct Tasmanians. We further hold that this primary element passed as full-blood Papuasians in extremely remote, possibly late Pliocene or early Pleistocene times, into Tasmania, while that island was still connected with the mainland, and the mainland, through New Guinea, with Malaysia. By the subsidence of the Austral land connections the Tasmanians were cut off from all contact with other races, and thus remained to the last *full-blood Papuasians*, somewhat modified by long isolation in a new and more temperate environment.

Meanwhile by the still persisting, northern land-connection, Australia was invaded by a people of unknown stock, possibly akin to the Dravidians of India, or to the Veddahs of Ceylon, or to the Toalas of Celebes, and these intruders gradually merged with the Papuasian aborigines in the hybrid race which we now call Australians. Lastly, there was a very much later and slighter Malayan graft, which was confined to the northern or north-western districts, and can be established on linguistic, cultural and even physical grounds.

The whole argument was fully developed by Mr Mathew roughly on these lines, first in *The Australian Aborigines (Jour. R. Soc. N.-S.*

Wales, 1889), and again still more thoroughly in *Eaglehawk and Crow*, 1899. But although well received in some quarters and favourably noticed in the *Geographical Journal* (XVI. p. 229), *The Academy, The Saturday Review, Notes and Queries*, and elsewhere, this work was treated in a step-motherly fashion by some of the leading authorities in Australian ethnology, notably the late Dr A. W. Howitt, blindly followed by Mr N. W. Thomas and M. A. Van Gennep. Not only were his general views strangely misrepresented, and his linguistic data absolutely caricatured, but he himself was regarded as a *novus homo*, a mere amateur in this branch of anthropological studies. It seems therefore desirable, in order to put matters on a right footing, here to give a few personal notes, which Mr Mathew might not himself care to supply, but which are none the less needed to establish his competency to deal with these matters, on which he is in fact immeasurably better informed than any of his opponents, Dr Howitt alone excepted.

For Mr Mathew Australian origins, languages, traditions, religion, folk-lore and social
usages have been a life study, and the knowledge bearing upon these questions, which most
others have gleaned from the library shelves,
he has acquired at first hand in the native
camping-grounds. While still in his teens he
was brought into the closest contact with the
aborigines on his uncle's station in Queensland,
where the Kabi dialect became for him almost
a second mother-tongue. At an early date
he prepared an account of that tribe, which
was embodied in Mr Curr's big work on *The
Australian Race*, and it was by living in their
midst that he detected in the original stock the
evidence of a blend with a straight-haired
people, such as the proto-Dravidians might
have been.

Then, after a thorough training in the
Natural Sciences under the late Sir F. M'Coy
at Melbourne University, including Comparative Anatomy, Zoology, and Palæontology, and
after reading nearly everything that has been

written of value on Australian anthropology, he might well complain that some of his would-be critics had rated him "just a little too cheaply."

The author, in the present work, aims at a serious discussion of contested questions, as in the chapters upon Kinship and Marriage, Social Organisation, Magic and Religion, Myths and Legends. Special attention has been paid to the linguistic side of the argument, on which Mr Mathew can speak with unquestioned authority. It will be noticed that, with other competent observers, he rejects a Negrito element in the constitution of the Australian race, and in support of that view it may here be pointed out that for the assumed kinship of the Austro-Tasmanian languages with that of the Andamanese Negritos there is no evidence whatever. As we now know from the studies of E. H. Man and R. C. Temple, Andamanese is a surprisingly intricate form of speech, characterised by an absolutely bewildering superfluity of pronominal and other formative elements. Thus the possessive pronouns have as many as sixteen possible variants, according to the class of noun (human objects, parts of the body, degrees of kinship, irrational things, and so on) with which they are in agreement. *My*, for instance, becomes *dia, dot, dong, dig, dab, dar, daka, doto, ad, ad-en, deb,* with *man, head, wrist, mouth, father, son, step-son, wife,* etc. Then there is a rank growth of agglutinated postfixes, so that "in adding their affixes they follow the principles of the ordinary agglutinative tongues ; in adding their prefixes they follow the well-defined principles of the South African tongues. Hitherto, as far as I know, the two principles in full play have never been found together in any other language. In Andamanese both are fully developed, so much so as to interfere with each other's grammatical functions" (Temple). Such an extraordinary system may betray certain analogies with the African Bantu family, but has nothing in common with the simply agglutinating Australian or Tasmanian languages.

On the general relations of speech to race
Mr Mathew has some judicious remarks which
may be here supported by what I have elsewhere written on this interesting subject:
"The statement that language proves social
contact only, and is no aid to the ethnologist,
implies a fundamental misconception of the
correlation of speech to race. Cases may and
do arrive where language will infallibly prove
the presence of distinct ethnical elements
which, but for it, would never have even been
suspected, much less determined. In Europe
a case in point are the Basques, shown by
their speech to be at least partly descended
from a pre-Aryan or a non-Aryan race, which
has elsewhere apparently disappeared, but has
far more probably become amalgamated with
the intruding Aryan peoples. . . . A Malay
element in the Negroid peoples of Madagascar
is placed beyond doubt by their Malayo-
Polynesian dialects. Or are we to suppose
that by crossing from the African mainland
to the neighbouring island, the Mozambique

b

Bantus forgot their mother-tongue, and began
to speak Malay, somehow wafted with the trade-
winds across the Indian Ocean to Madagascar?
Language, used with judgment, is thus seen to
be a great aid to the ethnologist in determining
racial affinities, and in solving many anthropological difficulties." (*Ethnology*, pp. 204-5.)

And so Mr Mathew is justified in contend-
ing for a slight strain of Malay blood in some
Australian groups from the slight traces of
Malay language in their speech. No doubt it
is argued that these Malay words, or some of
them, are also common to the Polynesians and
other Oceanic peoples. But what then?
Surely such terms do not cease to be Malay
because they form part of the great Oceanic
(Malayo-Polynesian) linguistic family. As
well maintain that *crown* is not an English
word because it derives through Norman
French from the Latin *corona!* Unless used
cautiously and with some knowledge of philological principles, language is a dangerous
pitfall, and into that pitfall Mr Curr hopelessly

fell when he tried to establish a kinship between the Australian and the African tongues. It is much to the credit of Mr Mathew that, at first following in the wake of Mr Curr, he stopped short in time, avoided the pitfall, and arrived at sane conclusions regarding the true relations of the Austro-Tasmanian tongues. The same remark, without pursuing the argument further, applies also to most of his other conclusions on the general ethnical and social relations of the Australian aborigines.

A. H. KEANE.

PREFACE

" THE inhabitants of the continent of Australia have long been a puzzle to ethnologists." Thus wrote Sir W. H. Flower in his *Essays on Museums*.

Ethnologists seem to be approaching a close agreement on the origin of the Australians, and it is my hope that this volume, not only in the Inquiry, Chap. I., but also in other parts, will contribute to a fuller solution of the " puzzle."

For over six consecutive years up to 1872 I lived in the country of the Kabi tribe and was in constant touch with Kabi and Wakka natives. Subsequently I was in occasional touch with them until 1876, when I removed to Melbourne. I renewed my acquaintance by a three months' visit in 1884, and in October 1906 I again visited the Kabi territory and interviewed natives.

Dr Howitt has written about these Kabi people under the name of Kaiabara. This is merely a local term by which only a few families claiming a small area as their common home would be known. Others have followed Dr Howitt in this misnomer. The people, constituted one tribe by community of language, and conscious of their unity, call themselves and their language Kabi.

Since writing my sketch of the Kabi tribe for Curr's *The Australian Race*,[1] I have, through correspondence and by means of personal intercourse with aborigines, collected additional information, some of it of exceptional importance. It seemed to me, therefore, advisable to embody in a monograph all I had learned about the Kabi and Wakka tribes, presenting the material in a separate book, and in a form as complete as possible.

The increasing interest and importance attaching to anthropological research, and especially to Australian problems, are, I think,

' Vol. iii. pp. 152-209.

sufficient justification for the publication of a work like this, which gives at first hand a much fuller and a more accurate account of these two tribes than is available elsewhere.

I desire to acknowledge my obligation to the following for assistance rendered :   To the Queensland Aborigines' Protection Department, for furthering my inquiries ; to Mr B. J. T. Lipscombe specially, Superintendent of Barambah Aboriginal Settlement, for collecting and verifying information ; to Mr J. Steven of Toromeo, Queensland, for photos and information ; to Rev. and Mrs J. H. Stähle of Condah, Victoria, for help in prosecuting investigation ; and, finally, to Prof. A. H. Keane, for perusal of the manuscript, his valuable suggestions and his generous Introduction.

JOHN MATHEW.

The Manse,
Coburg, Victoria, 1910.

TWO REPRESENTATIVE TRIBES OF QUEENSLAND

CHAPTER I

INQUIRY CONCERNING THE ORIGIN OF THE AUSTRALIAN RACE

A FORMER work, *Eaglehawk and Crow*, dealt with the Australian aborigines as a whole. In it I discussed the larger questions of their origin and distribution, and made a survey of the languages which embraced an original classification. My work obtained, for the most part, as favourable a reception as I could have expected.

A difficulty I had to face was to find a term which might suitably include Papuans, Melanesians, autochthonous Australians and Tasmanians. Differences of nomenclature among previous writers embarrassed me, some using Papuan, others Melanesian, as the more comprehensive name. I adopted Papuan.

One primary aim I had in view was to make my work, as far as possible, an original contribution to the solution of Australian problems. This principle led me to restrict my borrowing of materials and accounts for the large space given to philological discussion. I am able to speak one Australian language, and had studied the whole field of Australian languages, and was therefore able to comment upon them and draw conclusions from them at first hand.

I have been blamed for attaching too much weight to linguistic evidence. I acknowledge that I might have placed less stress upon linguistic resemblances as proof of racial affinity. But it should be observed that, while fifty years ago or more, when Bopp and Max Müller were founding the science of comparative philology, the tendency was to lean too much upon language in ethnological research, the present tendency is to lean too little upon it. Linguistic features are exceedingly persistent, and they cannot pass from one place to another without the contact of human beings to transmit them.

The well-marked and comparatively numerous analogies that connect the Tasmanian languages with those of Victoria, the respective inhabitants of the two countries having been absolutely separated for many thousands of years, form a pertinent illustration. Prof. Keane, referring to Mr Sidney H. Ray's ethnological investigations in New Guinea, characterises the case as "one of those instances in which speech proves to be not merely a useful, but also an indispensable factor in determining the constituent elements of mixed races." [1]

In the Australian languages the modifications of words can be traced, I maintain, by comparing their form in different dialects. The dialects may be likened to successive geological deposits or to chronological sequences in the literature of written languages.

I claim to have been the first to have given convincing proof that congeners of the Tasmanians were the true autochthones of Australia. I did this in an essay, published

[1] *Ethn.*, p. 287.

in the *Proceedings of the Roy. Soc. of N.-S. Wales*, in 1889. Linguistic affinities formed, perhaps, the strongest part of the evidence. But the cogency of this evidence has been acknowledged, and my conclusion as to the relation of the Tasmanians to the Australians has not been challenged by any of my critics. It is gratifying to me to know that my theory of the origin of the Australians is endorsed in the main by so eminent an anthropologist as Prof. A. H. Keane.[1]

The following is a brief statement of my theory :—

The ancestors of the now extinct Tasmanians were the original inhabitants of Australia. They were a short, black, or very dark brown, curly-haired race, congeners of the Papuans and Melanesians. But, unlike these two races, the Tasmanians, being absolutely separated from higher races, made virtually no advance in culture. At a time when Tasmania formed part of the mainland, or was much more easily accessible from it than in historic times, it was occupied by the then Australian race. There would not necessarily be absolute uniformity

[1] *Ethn.*, p. 290 *et seq.* and *Man Past and Pres.*, pp. 145-6.

in physical characters and language among the primitive race in all places. There would be some differences, and these would probably be graduated from south to north so as to approximate to the Melanesians. Owing to the formation or enlargement of Bass Strait by a subsidence of the land, Tasmania and its inhabitants became isolated from the mainland and its people. The Tasmanians remained physically and mentally in their primitive condition. A superior race, akin perhaps to the Dravidians of India, the Veddahs of Ceylon and the Toalas of Celebes, though not necessarily derived from one of these lands, migrated into Australia from the north-east. The newcomers were straight-haired and, though dark in complexion, were not so dark as their predecessors. They pressed forward, gradually absorbing or exterminating the lowlier, earlier inhabitants, until they overran the whole of Australia, the true autochthones leaving more traces of their presence in some places than in others. The vestiges of the Tasmanians were more pronounced in Victoria, which is shown by the fact that the Victorian dialects contain a considerable number of pure Tasmanian words. The Australians of historic times are therefore a hybrid race, constituted mainly of the Tasmanian and Asiatic elements. This fusion is indicated by the physical affinities of the Australians with the Tasmanians on the one hand and with the aborigines of Central India on the other.

I further suggest that the two races are represented by the two primary classes, or phratries, of Australian society, which were generally designated by names indicating a contrast of colour, such as eaglehawk and crow. The crow, black cockatoo, etc., would represent the Tasmanian element; the eaglehawk, white cockatoo, etc., the so-called Dravidian.

I also affirm a comparatively recent, slight infusion of Malay blood in the northern half of Australia. If, in accordance with recent conclusions, Indonesians must be distinguished from Malays, a point on which I am incompetent to judge, then I would say that both Malays and Indonesians have affected the Australian people in the north.

In addition, there seem to me to be hints of Melanesian influence among the tribes on and near the east coast, but, as the evidence is slight, I do not press this point.

Adopting as a general name the term "Papuasians," suggested to me by Prof. A. H. Keane, the relation of the Australians to the contiguous races may thus be indicated :—

Papuasians
{
Papuans proper,
Melanesians,
Tasmanians, including earliest Australians.
}

The Papuasians may have been developed from the Negrito up to a certain stage in one line. A Dravidian infusion was added to the Australian Papuasian and later a Malay, *Dravidian being used as a term of convenience.*

The theory of the origin of the Australian race which I have just sketched has been aptly designated "the Conflict Theory."

Since the publication of *Eaglehawk and Crow*, fresh evidence has come to light to support this theory and to corroborate my suggestion that the two great Australian classes represent the original conflicting races.

Mrs Langloh Parker has discovered that the names of the two great divisions or phratries among the Euahlayi (Gwaigulleah and Gwaimudthen) mean respectively *light-blooded* and *dark-blooded*.[1]

Mrs D. M. Bates, of Perth, West Australia, has also made the discovery that the classes there correspond to distinctions in the colour of the skin (light and dark), and that the aborigines claim to be able to distinguish the classes by their physical features. In a letter dated 12th April 1907, she says: "That the classes represent types, as you say, and are the coalescence of different races, there is no doubt. The Tondarup have a name expressive of their fairness, mela murnong (fair people), also the Ballaruks have a name ngwoota murnong (dark-skinned people)."

And quite unexpectedly, when I visited Barambah, in the country of the Kabi tribe, Queensland, in October 1906, I discovered to my great surprise, that not only were the two phratries recognised as representing re-

[1] She says : "The first division among the tribe is a blood distinction ('phratries') :—Gwaigulleah (*light-blooded*), Gwaimudthen (*dark-blooded*). This distinction is not confined to the human beings of the tribe, who must be of one or the other, but there are the Gwaigulleah and the Gwaimudthen divisions in all things."—*The Euah. Tr.*, p. 11.

spectively *light-blood* and *dark-blood* people, but the distinction carried with it the idea of corresponding difference in the colour of the skin, and a great part, if not the whole, of animated nature was embraced in this colour distinction.

I would direct the reader's attention also to the conflict myths, which I obtained at the same time (the farthest north that they have as yet been discovered), showing clearly the reference to the primeval antagonism of the eagle-hawk and the crow.

There is still further confirmation of the theory of the identity of the phratries and the two races.   On visiting recently two aboriginal reserves in Victoria, Condah and Coranderrk, five natives, one of whom was close on eighty and the others over sixty years of age, told me, when interrogated separately, that the old blacks professed to be able to distinguish members of the Kurokaity from those of the Kapaity phratry, and members of the Bundyil from those of the Wa by the quality of the hair.   Two told me that one phratry had fine hair, the other coarse.   And, corroborative of this distinction, a sixth native, belonging to

Swan Hill on the Murray, taking hold of his hair, said, " I'm kīrlba (*straight hair*), other fellows are mŏkwar (*curly hair*)," and went on to explain that the *straight-hair* people could not marry among themselves but had to inter-marry with the *curly-hair* people, and *vice versa*. This information would have fallen on deaf ears had I not known that Kīlpara and Mŏkwara were the names of the phratries over nearly all the western half of New South Wales.   I had hitherto associated these names with the birds eaglehawk and crow, as others had done, but here was an unexpected dis-covery of a quite different application of the stems of these terms.   On the Darling the name for eaglehawk, is bīlyara ; and for crow, waku.   I have examined many vocabularies but in none have I found names for these birds like the Darling phratry names, Kīlpara and Mŏkwara.   It is therefore probable that eagle-hawk and crow are only secondary applications of these terms, and the evidence above cited renders it also probable that the more special application, perhaps even the radical signifi-cance, is, straight-haired and curly-haired.

The distinction of sluggish blood and swift

blood is said to be recognised by the Itchmundi, Murawari, Wonghibon and Ngeumba tribes of New South Wales. According to Mr R. H. Mathews, these qualities of blood do not refer to the phratries but to sections, presumably independent of them.[1] Still his names for the two bloods are the same as those given by Mrs Langloh Parker as applied to the Euahlayi phratries. Possibly Mr R. H. Mathews' instance represents a later development which recognises an admixture of the bloods. His "shades" recall the gradations which are found in the Kabi and Wakka tribes, but in them the four gradations of colour correspond to the four classes. Mr N. W. Thomas shows that the names of the blood organisation and the phratry organisation appear to be inextricably intermingled in the accounts of the four New South Wales tribes and the adjoining tribes as given by Mr R. H. Mathews and Dr Howitt.[2]

That the classes stand for blood-distinctions is far from being a new idea. It was entertained by Leichhardt, Bunce and others.[3]

---

[1] *Ethn., Notes*, p. 7 *et seq.*
[2] *Kin. and Mar. in Austr.*, p. 50.
[3] Bunce's *Lang. of the Abor.*, etc., 1859, p. 58.

The foregoing evidence should suffice to prove that the blood distinctions are real, and must strengthen the hypothesis that they originally corresponded to racial differences.

Those who have discussed the origin of the Australians, have usually given an outline of the theories of preceding authors. I have done this already in my former work.[1] It is rendered the less necessary for me to go over this ground now, since it has been traversed by the three most recent writers on the subject, viz., the late Dr Howitt,[2] M. Arnold Van Gennep,[3] and Mr N. W. Thomas.[4] Referring to the views of these writers in reverse order, that of Mr Thomas seems to be almost identical with Dr Howitt's, and, if so, does not differ greatly from my own.[5] I say *seems to be*, because his language, in places, is so undecided that it is difficult to know what he is prepared to commit himself to. Thus, he seems to favour Flower and Lydekker's view, that the Australian is of Melanesian *cum* Caucasian Melanochroi origin, then, following Ling Roth,

---

[1] *Eag. and Cr.*, pp. 1-5.   [2] *Nat. Tr. of S.-E. Aust.*
[3] *Myt. et Leg. D'Austr.*   [4] *Nat. of Aust.*
[5] *Ibid.*, pp. 12-18.

he favours affinities of the Tasmanians with
the Andamans, then he speaks of the *Negrito*
population of West Australia, and finally says :
" There is no need to discard the Negrito-
Caucasic hypothesis." [1] All this is rather loose,
vague, and confusing, unless Melanesians, or
Tasmanians, or both, are to be called Negritos,
which, I submit, they ought not to be. Further,
he thinks probable, a modern Papuan infiltration in the north of Australia, and a Malay
strain in the north and north-west. He finds
a stumbling-block in the way of the hypothesis
that Tasmania was peopled from Victoria, in
the, by him, alleged fact, that, in Victoria, man
has left " no traces which can, by any possi-
bility, go back as far as to antedate the
Caucasian immigration." I hold that no such
stumbling-block exists since my demonstration
of the affinities of the Tasmanian language
with the Victorian dialects.[2]

M. Arnold Van Gennep discredits all theories
of Australian origin.[3] My main defect, he
says, is confusing notions of race, culture,
and language, which ought to be dissociated.

[1] *Nat. of Aust.*, p. 14.   [2] *Eag. and Cr.*, pp. 39-41.
[3] *Myt. et Leg.*, *Intro.*

" L'observation directe," he says, "l'enseigne." [1]
No doubt.   But one may recognise the differences without making a distinct, threefold
classification.   As a matter of fact, in treating
of the relation between the Tasmanians and
the Australians, I separate physical characters
from other evidence and deal with them first
of all.   A neglected child, in Melbourne, was
allowed to play with the fowls in the backyard.
She acquired their habits in eating, fighting,
etc., their language in crowing, etc., but she
was no fowl.   So, as regards branches of the
human   race,   culture   is   easily   transmitted,
language less easily, while physical characters
in common necessarily imply genealogical relationship, allowing for aberrations which cannot
be taken into account.   Similarity in language
in the case of savage races, especially if they
are far apart and have been long disconnected,
must always count for much as evidence of
racial affinity.   But physical characters are
easily of first importance, and biologists would
assist anthropology immensely, if they would
decide the relative importance of particular
features.

[1] *Myt. et Leg., Intro.*, p. vi.

M. Van Gennep also objects to my referring
to the Malays as a *race*. Anthropologists
generally admit the vagueness of the word
race. But competent authorities affirm a
Malay type. Keane quotes several writers in
support of this view.[1] I certainly have not
distinguished between Malays and Indonesians,
although there appear grounds for so doing.
There was the less necessity, for my purpose,
to make the distinction, if, with Deniker, we may
regard Indonesians as of the purest Malay type.[2]

M. Van Gennep unintentionally creates a
wrong impression when he says that Dr Howitt
has demolished in detail my linguistic evidence.[3]
Dr Howitt merely objects to my calling Malay
three words which I cite, on the ground that
Codrington gives them as not exclusively
Malay, but as belonging to the Oceanic mother-
tongue. As regards his own view of the
Australians, he says : "The craniological characters of this race relate it on the one hand
to the pithecanthrope, on the other to the Spy
Neanderthal." "The varied Australian differences resemble some other living types,

[1] *Ethn.*, p. 330.   [2] *Races of Man*, p. 487.
[3] *Myt. et Leg.*, p. vi.

Dravidians, Veddas, Ainus, groups of North Africa and probably of Europe, but the real relationship of these varieties with one or other of the groups remains to be determined." [1] This is almost like saying, the Australians resemble all races, past and present, but more than that nobody knows. Surely we have reached greater definiteness than this.

The theory of Schoetensack, mentioned by Van Gennep, that, in Australia, all the human varieties were formed, which in succession have spread over the globe,[2] cannot be seriously entertained, in the face of obvious facts.

The conclusions of Dr Klaatsch, who recently visited Australia, I shall give in his own words. He says : " I agree with Turner [3] in his views of

---

[1] *Myt. et Leg.*, p. xxii.   [2] *Ibid.*, p. x.

[3] Sir W. Turner's most recently expressed opinion, as published in the *Scotsman* of 7th July 1908, is opposed to that of Dr Klaatsch and is apparently in harmony with mine. He is reported thus : " The idea of resemblance broke down in the case of the Tasmanians and the existing Australians. But might not Australia have been occupied by a race prior to the race that now formed the native population ; and when Australia and Tasmania were joined to each other by land, could not that race have found their way to Tasmania and remained there, whereas the same race had apparently disappeared from Australia." " He thought the term Negritto ought to be limited to those dwarf people with strongly brachycephalic skulls."

the unitary nature of the Australian race.   I do
not believe that the variations, many of which
are additional to those mentioned by him, have
anything to do with the crossing of different
races.[1]   He approves of the suggestion of
Ch. H. Barton, that the Australian aboriginal
population has not been derived from any
other at present existing region, but is rather
to be regarded as "coeval with the continent
itself."   Again he says : "I agree with Turner
that there is at present no proof of the existence of different races on the Australian
continent."[2]   "We have the Tasmanians as a
type, which doubtless emerged from the same
root as the Australian, and has become very
distinct through local isolation."[3]   "There has
been time and room enough to effect local
specialisations in the primitive unitary type,
which must be accepted as the common root
from whence sprung all the Australian and
Tasmanian people."[3]

Dr Klaatsch's conclusions are entitled to
very great respect but, it seems to me, that he

---

[1] *Reps. from the Path. Lab. of the Lun. Dept. of N.-S.W.
Govt.* (1908), p. 159.
[2] *Ibid.*, p. 149.   [3] *Ibid.*, p. 150.

B

closes his eyes to certain kinds of evidence as if they were of no consequence.

He says he failed to get the information he asked for as to the authority of osteologists for the Australians being a hybrid people. The subjoined extracts should be ample authority.

E. H. Giglioli, *I Tasmaniani*, p. 146. Milano, 1874. (The translations are mine).

"I agree exactly with the final opinion expressed by Blanchard, according to which it is possible to define the aborigine of Tasmania as an Australian having Papuan hair. . . . They were probably remnants of a black woolly-haired race of New Holland, preserved a little longer because their land had become an island. . . . The Tasmanians were therefore ancient members, a little modified, of the great Papuasian family, and owed their inferiority to the state of complete isolation in which they had lived from a remote epoch."

Archivio per l'Antrop., XXIV., 1894. (Quoted by Keane in his *Ethnology*, p. 289.)

"I observe finally that the Tasmanians were Negroid and different from the Australians, whom I consider degenerated Aryans."

Topinard, *Anthropology*, p. 502 (Eng. Ed.), 1890.

"It is clear that the Australians might very well be a

cross between one race, with smooth hair, from some other place, and a really negro and autochthonous race. The opinions expressed by Huxley are in harmony with this hypothesis. He says the Australians are identical with the ancient inhabitants of the Deccan."

While, like Giglioli, not asserting he leaves the question of a crossing of races, Topinard yet enumerates eight Indian races, including the Veddahs, whom he says might be considered as *of the same race* as the Australians.

Huxley and Topinard therefore both un-equivocally relate the Australians to the people of the Deccan. Topinard certainly does not affirm that the negroid element is descended from congeners of the Tasmanians but, ad-mitting the earlier occupation of Australia by the progenitors of the Tasmanians, it is a legitimate inference from Topinard's state-ments, when viewed in the light of other evidence, that the cross was between one race of the same stock as the Tasmanians and another of the same stock as the Dravidians.

Flower and Lydekker, *An Introduction to the Study of Mammals, Living and Extinct*, p. 748.   London, 1891.

"Australia may have been originally peopled with

frizzly-haired Melanesians . . . but a strong infusion of some other race, probably a low form of Caucasian Melanochroi, such as that which still inhabits the interior of the southern parts of India, has spread throughout the land from north-west and produced a modification of the physical characters, especially of the hair."

(*See* also Flower's *Essays on Museums*, pp. 280-281).

When therefore Dr Klaatsch declares so emphatically and confidently against a fusion of races in Australia, he is knocking his head against experts in biology and not merely against writers like Dr Howitt and myself.

There are certain facts in Australian ethnology which cannot be ignored in the problem of the origin of the race, and which the views of Dr Klaatsch fail to account for. One fact is the extreme divergence in the quality of the hair, from straightness like that of the Hindu to frizziness like the Melanesian's. Along with this is the almost universal prevalence of the bisection of society accompanied by the conviction that the sections are of different kin or blood and, in some places, by the divisions being distinguished as straight-haired and curly-haired, light-blooded and dark-blooded, fair-skinned and dark-skinned. An indication of the deep and radical character of this bisection is supplied by the fact that in the west of Victoria and the contiguous part of South Australia, on the occasions of the *kuyurn*, or intertribal conference, and intertribal corroborees, the two phratries, Kurokaity and Kapaity, were absolutely segregated, the members of the one, young and old of both sexes, keeping apart from those of the other except when retiring to sleep. Spencer and Gillen mention the same custom as prevailing in Central Australia. Then there is the distribution of the types of language, all radiating from Cape York peninsula, and there are the evidences that culture has travelled from the north. As an illustration, take the case of the people in the south-west corner of Australia. By language and social organisation they are closely connected with the people of North-Central Queensland. There can be no doubt that at some remote period they crossed the continent from north-east to south-west. Facts like these Dr Klaatsch and his theory simply take no cognisance of.

Dr Howitt differs from me in his views about

the racial affinities of the Tasmanians. I hold that they were most closely allied to the Papuans and Melanesians. Above I have grouped them with these two races under Papuasians. Dr Howitt adopts Mr Ling Roth's conclusion as expressed in the first edition of his *Aborigines of Tasmania*, "That the Tasmanians were more closely related to the Andaman Islanders than to any other race." The evidence which Roth relied upon, so far as it goes or is of any value, leads me to a different conclusion from his. Let us look at his evidence.

In Chapter XIII. of Roth's work, Dr J. G., Garson gives the results of a careful study of the skeletal characters of the Tasmanians. Four only of the comparisons he makes are relevant to our inquiry, as they alone refer equally to Tasmanians, Andamanese and Melanesians.

1. The Sacral Index, measured by Prof. Flower,[1]

4 male Tasmanians,		100.7
17 ,,	New Caledonians,	101
8 ,,	Andamanese,	94

[1] Roth's *Abor. of Tasm.*, p. 208 *et seq.*

2. The Brim Index—

> Tasmanian,   93.1
> New Caledonian,   94.6
> Andamanese,   98.8

Dr Garson says the Tasmanian pelvis "agrees very closely in all its important measurements with the New Caledonian."[1]

3. Antibrachial Index—

> Tasmanian,   79.9 in males, 78.1 in females.
> New Caledonian,   76.6   „   75.8   „
> Andamanese,   81.7   „   80.6   „

4. Tibiofemoral Index—

> Tasmanian,   84.1 in males, 79.1 in females.
> New Caledonian,   83.1   „   82.3   „
> Andamanese,   84.4   „   84.4   „

At first sight this fourth comparison suggests a closer affinity between Tasmanian and Andamanese than between the former and New Caledonians. But the Andamanese measurement is an average for males and females. Striking averages for the Tasmanians and New Caledonians gives 81.6 for the former and 82.7 for the latter, as compared with 84.4 in the Andamanese.

[1] Roth's *Abor. of Tasm.*, p. 210 (Sec. Ed.).

Thus, in three out of the four comparisons tabled, the Tasmanian measurements agree much more closely with the New Caledonian (Melanesian), than with the Andamanese. This is the sole relevant osteological evidence adduced, and it should be noted that Dr Garson's conclusion is not identical with Mr Roth's. Dr Garson says : " In some respects the Tasmanians very closely resemble the Negrito race, not only in the character of their hair but in some of their osteological characters. . . . The Melanesian race has by many persons been claimed as that to which the Tasmanians are most nearly allied, and many of their physical characters support this hypothesis." [1]

This surely means that the Tasmanians resembled the Melanesians more than they did the Negritos, and if so, then Mr Roth's conclusion " That the Tasmanians were more closely allied to the Andaman Islanders than to any other race," is contrary to Dr Garson's evidence.

In the *second* edition Mr Roth is not so specific. While still regarding the Tasmanians

[1] Roth's *Abor. of Tasm.*, p. 210 (Sec. Ed.).

as having closely resembled the Negritos, he omits his former conclusion (just quoted) and therefore does not press so close an affinity to the Andamans as he did in the first edition.

I offer no objection to Prof. Flower's theory that the Negroes and negroid races of Oceania may have been developed from the Negrito race. I think it very probable that Melanesians, Papuans and Tasmanians may have emerged from a Negrito stock. But, I submit, that there is a tendency to use the term Negrito too loosely. If we are to adhere to the radical meaning of the word, we should apply it only to the black, curly or woolly-haired, dwarf races. It is a loose application of the term that makes it embrace the Melanesians and Tasmanians, some even of the latter having exceeded six feet in height. Topinard, more consistently, calls the Tasmanians Negroes and the Andamanese Negritos.

The opinion, which I have long held, is that Australia, New Guinea and Melanesia were originally inhabited by one and the same race, which was represented in its most primitive form by the Tasmanians. These remained unprogressive while the Papuans and Melanesians advanced considerably, through contact with the Polynesians, and perhaps at some points with the Malays.   This opinion may be impossible of proof.   It involves, perhaps, the inference that the Melanesian language as now prevailing has been superimposed upon a language like the Tasmanian.

To come now to the evidence from hair adduced by Mr Roth.   Dr Sydney J. Hickson made a comparative study for him of the hair of Tasmanians, Australians, Andamanese and Papuans of the south coast.[1]   He says that the hair of the Tasmanians is of a light golden-brown colour, that it is finer than the hair of the Papuans and Australians, but not so fine as the hair of the Andamanese, that it is less curly than that of any of the Papuans or Andamanese, but more so than that of the Australians, the average diameters of the curls being :

Andamanese	2 mm.
Papuan	3 mm.
Tasmanian	5 mm.
Australian	15 mm.

The hairs of the Tasmanians are also said to

[1] Roth's *Abor. of Tasm.*, p. 221.

be flatter than those of the Australians and Papuans.

The first great defect noticeable about the argument from the hair is that we have no comparison at all made between Tasmanian and Melanesian hair. Further, even if we allow the Papuans to represent the Melanesians in this case, as regards the curliness of the hair, the Papuans come nearer to the Andamanese than do the Tasmanians.

Then, as to colour, one wonders how many samples of Tasmanian hair Dr Hickson examined when he pronounced it a light, golden-brown colour. If he only had one sample or a very few samples, the hair would appear to have been very exceptional, for while there might be, as among the Australians, an occasional fair-haired person or family among the Tasmanians, the concurrence of testimony is that their hair was black. Thus R. Brough Smith quotes from Cook's diary about the Tasmanians : " Their skin was black and also their hair." [1]   He also quotes Mr R. H. Davies : " Their hair is black and woolly." [2]   In a paper on the aborigines of Tasmania, read before the

[1] *Abor. of Vic.*, vol. ii. p. 379.   [2] *Ibid.*

Australian Association for the Advancement of Science, which met at Melbourne in 1890, Mr James Barnard, Vice-President of the Royal Society of Tasmania, said : " The men allowed their hair, which was black and woolly, to grow very long, etc." [1]   And Mr Bonwick, who has been the most prolific writer on the Tasmanians, says : " The Tasmanian hair was black." [2]   Dr Barnard Davis characterised their hair as dark brown.   Prof. Berry and Dr Robertson of Melbourne have recently examined all available skulls in Tasmania, and they have found that the hair still adhering is black.

In the face of such testimony, how can we believe that the colour of the Tasmanian hair was generally a light golden-brown, or that, if Dr Hickson examined hair of that colour, it was an average sample ?

It seems, therefore, that the argument based on the character of the hair has very little bearing, if any, upon whether the Tasmanian is more closely allied to the Andamanese or the Melanesian.

The only other evidence Mr Roth relies

[1] *Proc. Assoc. for the Adv. of Sc.*, vol. ii. p. 598.
[2] *Daily Life of Tasm.*, p. 109.

upon is the linguistic. He cites not a single
word common to both languages. He quotes
Dr Fr. Müller as to the peculiar characteristics
of the Andamanese language, and goes on to
say that the Tasmanian language "is agglutinating with suffixes and apparently also with
prefixes in its word construction, and wanting
in those hisses and buzzes similarly wanting in
the Andamans."[1] From these generalities he
concludes that the Tasmanian language has
Andamanese affinities. He also makes the
following comparison—if it can be called a
comparison :—

Tasmanian Pers. Pron.
1st pers. sing., mi-na
2nd ,,   ,,   ni-na
3rd ,,   ,,   (narra)
Andamanese Poss. Pron.
sing., di-a,   plu., m-etat
  ,,   n-ia,   ,,   n-etat
  ,,   l-ia,   ,,   l-ontat.

He adds : " It is curious that the singular
case suffix among the Andamanese is — da,
while the Tasmanians used the syllable—na
for the same purpose."[2] That is the whole of
his linguistic evidence. What is it worth?

[1] *Abor. of Tasm.* p. 227 (Sec. Ed.).   [2] *Ibid.*, p. 223.

Nothing.   Mr Roth recognised no linguistic
affinities between the Tasmanian and Australian
languages.   In fact, his conclusion in the first
edition seemed to be, that there was little or no
affinity between the Australians and Tasmanians.
It is to his credit that he did not regard the
question of origin settled, and that in the second
edition he has fallen into line with those who
affirm that the Tasmanians were the true
aborigines of Australia, and that they were
partly annihilated, partly absorbed, by an
invading race. [1]

The Tasmanian word for the 3rd personal
pronoun singular, cited by Roth, tells in favour
of my contention.   " Nara " is the 3rd personal
pronoun plural in Melanesian, and the 3rd personal
pronoun both singular and plural in Tasmanian.
This can hardly be a casual coincidence.   The
very same word was the most common terminal
sign of the plural in nouns in the language of
the Booandik tribe of South Australia. [2]

It may be worth mentioning here, as bearing upon the point being dealt with, that the
words denoting *man* in several of the dialects

[1] *Abor. of Tasm.*, pp. 227-8 (Sec. Ed.).
[2] Mrs Smith's *Booandik Tr.*, p. 125.

in the east of Australia, have analogues in the Melanesian language. The following are examples :—

Australian	*Melanesian*
mari	mare
mean, main, mai-i	maani
woani	moana
maar, mara	ma
dhan	ata, ta

Words of this class in Australia are very important. They sometimes indicate a distinct dialect, sometimes they serve to subsume tribes, probably of common origin, that form a nation.

Other important words could be added to the above list, as for instance, "lai-yuruk," a common Victorian word for woman, the first syllable is identical with the Melanesian word "lai" (woman), but I refrain from citing more illustrations here.

I have shown that the evidence adduced by Mr Roth does not warrant his conclusion. I shall now show that certain very valuable evidence he has overlooked is very much against it.

He has attached no importance to difference of

stature.   The Andamanese are the tallest of the
Negritos, the average height of one hundred
and fifteen being, according to Deniker, 1.485 m.,
about 5 ft. 1½ in.[1]   Keane gives it as 4 ft. 10 in.[2]
Topinard, quoting from Hamy, gives it as a
little less, viz., 1.47 m.[3]   Deniker gives the
height of New Guinea Papuans as ranging
from 1.608 m. to 1.674 m., of Melanesians of
New Britain 1.62 m., and of New Caledonians
1.673 m.[4]   Topinard's figures for stature of
New Caledonians, after Bourgarel, are 1.67 m.[5]
None of these writers gives the height of the
Tasmanians.   In his work on the osteology
of the Tasmanians, Barnard Davies gives the
average height of three skeletons of males as
1.612 m., or 5 ft. 3½ in.   A little would require
to be added for the height when living.   Thus
in the case of twenty-three men, the average
was 5 ft. 3¾ in.   But among twenty-six measured
by Robinson at Port Davey in 1833, several
were 6 ft., and one Tasmanian, a murderer
named Cobia, was 6 ft. 2 in. in height.   Dr
Garson gauged the height in the living subject

[1] *Races of Man*, p. 577.   [2] *Ethn.*, p. 256.
[3] *Anthrop.*, p. 499.   [4] *Races of Man*, pp. 580-582.
                    [5] *Anthrop.*, p. 321.

to be about 1.661 m. The Tasmanians were therefore about the same height as the Melanesians of New Britain referred to above, and about 5 in. taller than the Andamanese. So far as stature goes, it is entirely in favour of a closer affinity with the Melanesians than with the Andamanese.

Another physical character regarded as important is the cephalic index. The following gives in columns the index supplied by different authors.

	Tasmanians.	Andamanese.	New Caledonians.	Papuans.
Keane,[1]	76.11	81.87	...	...
Deniker,[2]	74.9	81.6	70.7	74.2
Topinard,[3]	79.11	81.87	71.78	...
Barnard Davies,[4]	75.6	...	...	...

According to the above, the crania of the New Caledonians and Papuans are dolichocephalic, those of the Tasmanians dolichocephalic according to Deniker's figures, and sub-dolichocephalic according to the other writers, and the Andamanese crania are sub-brachycephalic. Keane says: "Sir W. Flower has placed it beyond all doubt that the typical

[1] *Ethn.*, p. 180.   [2] *Races of Man*, pp. 585-589.
[3] *Anthrop.*, pp. 240-242.   [4] *Ibid.*, p. 241.

C

58 Two Tribes of Queensland

Negritos are brachycephalous, the typical
Papuans dolichocephalous."[1] It will be
observed that according to this test the
Tasmanians stand about equally between the
New Caledonians and the Andamanese, but
come very close to the Papuans.

The following measurements of the orbital
index, taken by various writers, have been
given by Deniker.[2]

Tasmanians.	New Cale- donians.	Papuans.	Melanesians.	Andamanese.
80.8	80.6	84.4	85.1	91.7

The Tasmanians and Andamanese form the
extremes, and the New Caledonians, the purest
Melanesians, are, in this respect, practically
identical with the Tasmanians.

From a conjunct view of all the above comparisons, the natural inference surely must be
that the Tasmanians were much more closely
related to the Papuans and Melanesians than
to the Andamanese, and may reasonably be
placed as a third branch along with these in a
Papuasian group. This is in harmony with
Prof. Flower's opinion, published in 1878,
in his lecture in the Manchester series, where

[1] *Ethn.*, p. 178.　　[2] *The Races of Man*, p. 62.

he says: "The physical characters of the Tasmanians would appear to indicate that they are a branch of the Melanesian race, though modified in the course of long isolation." "The view then that I am most inclined to adopt is that they are derived from the same stock as the Papuans or Melanesians, that they reached Van Diemen's Land by way of Australia long anterior to the commencement of the comparatively high civilisation of those portions of the race still inhabiting New Guinea and the adjacent islands, and also anterior to the advent in Australia of the existing native race, characterised by the straight hair and by the possession of such weapons as the boomerang, the throwing - stick, and the shield." [1]

[1] True, Topinard has noted in the Tasmanian skeletal structure marked divergences from the Melanesian type. He remarks upon the cephalic index, the degree of prognathism, and the keel-shaped skull, in which particulars they differ, he says, from both the New Caledonians and the Australians and agree with the Polynesians. But I think he is in error in alleging that the keel - shaped skull is never found in Australians. Mr R. Brough Smith has figured the skull of King Jimmy of the Mordialloc tribe on p. 369, vol. ii., *The Aborigines of Victoria*, a glance at which will show that it is pronouncedly keel-shaped. In describing it Brough Smith says : "The sort of mid-rib running along the top of the skull,

Flower adheres to this view in his later works.[1]

By a different course of reasoning I had reached the same conclusions in 1889 as Prof. Flower, quite independently, having no knowledge then of his lecture nor of the somewhat similar theory of Prof. E. H. Giglioli, of Florence, published in 1874. And I submit that Roth's evidence, which seems to be accepted without examination by some subsequent writers, does not disturb the earlier view.

Exception has been taken by various writers to my having posited a slight infusion of Malay blood in the northern half of Australia. Dr Howitt, while not denying a very slight Malay influence, disagrees with me as to its extent. He would not have been wittingly unfair, but

like the crest of a gorilla, and bounded on each side by a temporal ridge, gives the skull a most ape-like appearance." After all, Topinard concludes his observations on the Tasmanian type by saying : "Their skulls in the Museum appeared to be a product between the Melanesian and the Polynesian." * This conclusion surely implies that physically the Tasmanians are more widely removed from the Andamans than from the Melanesians.

[1] *Introd. to the Study of Mammals*, p. 748 ; *Ess. on Mus.* (pub. 1898), pp. 280, 281.

* *Anthrop.*, p. 501.

he has done me an injustice in saying that I base
my conclusion on philological grounds alone,
and, that in addition to a comparison of interrogative pronouns, I have only twelve words to
rely upon.   On the authority of Codrington,
he affirms that three of these words are
common to the original stock of the Malay
and Melanesian languages.   This objection is
irrelevant.   If a thousand Malay words were
found in Australia, they might be disallowed
on exactly the same grounds as constituting
any evidence of a Malay strain in the
Australian race.

In *Eaglehawk and Crow* I adduced sixteen
words, of which all but two or three are certainly
Malay.   These Malay words may of course only
indicate a trifling trend of culture.   It would
have been absurd to have inferred from them
alone a Malay strain, as Dr Howitt alleges I
have done.   I distinctly state additional reasons
for my inference that in certain parts of the
northern half of Australia there has been an
infiltration of Malay blood.   I am amazed that
Dr Howitt should have ignored this, and that
he should be blindly followed by Mr N. W.
Thomas and M. Arnold Van Gennep.   Why,

the contents of my chapter on " The Malay
Element " include the following titles : Malay
activity, Physical appearance, Circumcision and
the message-stick of Malay introduction, and
yet Dr Howitt asserts that my Malayan
hypothesis rests first, on the identification of interrogative pronouns, and second, " on twelve
words, etc."[1]   He implies, although he does
not expressly affirm it, that I offer no other
evidence, and, on his authority, Thomas and
Van Gennep affirm categorically that I rely
on linguistic evidence alone.   Mr Thomas
exceeds Dr Howitt in his careless mis-
representation of the grounds on which I
infer a Malay element.   He says : " The
Rev. J. Mathew, on the other hand, finds
a Malay element in Australia, superposed
on the two earlier stocks ; but his arguments are entirely philological, and the
words on which he relies are selected at
random from different tribes : they are only
twelve in all, and the Malay words to which
they are traced back are not purely Malay,
but part of a common Oceanic language, in
existence long before Malays were ever heard

[1] *Nat. Tr. of S.-E. Austr.*, p. 25.

of." [1]   All this is merely an inaccurate exaggerated paraphrase of Dr Howitt's anim-
adversion, and shows that the writer gave
no independent thought to my Malayan
hypothesis.

It is scarcely consistent of Mr Thomas,
while ridiculing my citation of sixteen Malay
analogues, as part of my warrant for inferring
a Malay graft, to take up, at the same time,
about a page of his own book discussing the
bearing of a single word (which he does not
even name), the equivalent for water, upon
the connection of the Tasmanians with the
Australians.   Mr E. M. Curr states that in
Mr R. Brough Smyth's *Aborigines of Victoria*,
vol. i., p. lxx., a certain Mr R. H. Davies is
referred to as expressing the view that the
Tasmanians originally came from Australia and
part of them from Cape Leeuwin, and as
grounding his assertions on their agreement
in habits and weapons and on the equivalents
of the word for *water*.   Mr Curr shows that
there is not the slightest resemblance between
the Tasmanian words for water and Australian
words for the same object at or within a

[1] *Nat. of Austr.*, pp. 16-17.

hundred miles of Cape Leeuwin.   So that this
single word, that Mr Thomas gives so much
attention to, is a myth, and yet he says,
" possibly, therefore, the coincidence of the
word for water points to racial unity."

M. Arnold Van Gennep must next take up
the parable and tell his readers that Dr Howitt
has demolished in detail my linguistic evidence,
which, he also must assert, is my sole ground
for inferring Malay influence.

Far from my argument resting exclusively
upon the resemblance of a few words, I base it
also on physical features and culture.   I suggest
that the contrast in the physique of the people
in the north, as compared with those elsewhere,
is due to an admixture of Malays.   I affirm
the occurrence of faces of Malay type among
the Australians.   I point out that Grey saw
three men of a fair race resembling Malays,
who appeared to be leaders among the
aborigines, and that some of his men saw a
fourth.   This was near the cave where he saw
paintings of clothed people.   I lay stress upon
the maritime activity of the Malays and the
fact that from traces of old camps and the
appearance of old tamarind trees, Malays must

have been visiting the north-west coast for at least two hundred years. As regards culture, I refer the introduction of circumcision (arguing from the sphere of its prevalence) and the message-stick to Malays of Sumatra and I devote fourteen pages to a consideration of the rock paintings, the best of which I hold to have been executed by Lampong natives presumably domiciled in Australia. In spite of all this variety of evidence, certain writers coolly inform their readers that I rely only upon the resemblance of a few words.

The misunderstandings and misrepresentations which my theory of the origin of the Australians has suffered from, are, I think, sufficient excuse for my having taken so much trouble to meet objections, to re-state my theory, and to vindicate it. The present work, while much narrower in scope than *Eaglehawk and Crow*, will supply fresh evidence in support of my previous main conclusions.

In this discussion I have not brought forward arguments to prove that congeners of the Tasmanians, and no other race, formed the basal element in the Australian aborigines. For such arguments I refer readers to *Eagle-*

hawk and Crow, where I have marshalled them
—linguistic, cultural and physical—with considerable fulness.   I have thought it sufficient
at present to adduce additional proof that the
Australians are of hybrid origin, and I have
assumed that the curly-haired element was of
the same race as the Tasmanians.   Eminent
writers, like Topinard, Flower, and Lydekker,
have found sufficient reason to conclude that
one of the two original stocks that united to
form the Australian race might be Melanesian,
and I have been content now to essay the
proof that the Tasmanians were more closely
related to the Melanesians and Papuans than
to any other race, suggesting the inference
that if a Melanesian base be admitted for the
Australians, a Tasmanian base would be equally
admissible.

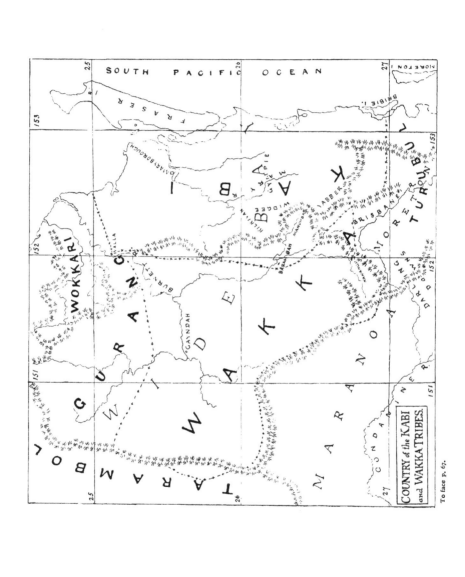

COUNTRY of the KABI and WAKKA TRIBES.

To face p. 67.

CHAPTER II

As is the case with nearly all the tribes in the east and south-east of Australia, the Kabi and Wakka tribes are so named from negatives in the respective dialects. The reason for this mode of nomenclature appears to be the fact that these negatives, by their frequent repetition, are more conspicuous to members of alien tribes than any other words. The Kabi people employ other negatives as well, viz., *wa* and *bar*, but *kabi* is distinctive of them.

The territory of the Kabi coincided approximately with the basin of the Mary River but extended along the coast beyond that basin both to the north and the south. Its coast-line extended from near the 27th parallel northward to about the mouth of the Burrum River, a distance of some 175 miles; measured across the land, the distance from point to point would be about 130 miles. The maximum width, measured westward from Double Island Point, is 85 miles.   In addition to the mainland, there was Fraser or Great Sandy Island, about 85 miles long with an average breadth of 12 miles, so that the Kabi country altogether had an area of about 8200 square miles.   I was informed by the blacks that at one time it embraced the whole of the bunya country.   If this were the case, encroachments had been made by neighbouring tribes on the west and south-west.

The people who spoke the dialect called Dippil by Rev. W. Ridley, his informant, apparently, being Davies, an escaped convict, belonged by all their characteristics to the Kabi tribe.   In fact his Dippil is just Kabi. But I have found no knowledge of the name Dippil among the Kabi people themselves, even on inquiring about it.

South of the Kabi, and having much in common with it, was the Turubul (Ridley) or Turrbal (Petrie) tribe of the Brisbane River. At the Kabi limits on the north, from the coast westward to Walla on the Burnett, the Wokkari tribe came in, and west of its territory the domain of the Gurang Gurang began.

The country of the Wakka Wakka lay to

the west of the Kabi. It took in a small part
of the Dawson basin, extended over a great
part of the basin of the Burnett, its boundary
passing eastward by about Coonambula, including Gayndah, and meeting the northern Kabi
boundary at Walla. It also included the upper
waters of the Brisbane, where it marched with
the Turubul. To the west of the Wakka the
Tarambol or Dawson River blacks were
located. The Wakka country was roughly
triangular in outline, the base running northward along the 152nd line of longitude from
Cooyar Creek on the south to Walla on the
Burnett, a distance of about 125 miles. The
perpendicular would run west near the 26th
parallel of latitude for a distance of about 80
miles, so that the area would be about 5000
square miles.

Although the Kabi and Wakka dialects are
largely distinct, especially as regards nouns
and adjectives, yet the two tribes followed
very much the same customs, they were very
friendly and intermarried freely, the class
restrictions being the same for both.

The territory of both tribes was generally
hilly. At the head waters of the Mary and

Brisbane Rivers it was mountainous and, in places, even picturesque. It was in almost all seasons well watered with flowing rivers and creeks, and the vegetation was abundant. In the Kabi country there are extensive scrubs, especially on the higher elevations, where there is a great variety of plant-life, one of the most beautiful and conspicuous features being the graceful bunya tree, the *Araucaria Bidwillii*. The kernels in the flakes of the cones of this tree formed a palatable, nutritious and plentiful food supply, and when the fruit was in season, other tribes were attracted from immense distances to enjoy Nature's bounty. The scrubs were the haunt of the wawun or scrub-turkey, known in Victoria as the Mallee hen.

The forest country was well wooded and abounded in marsupial game of several varieties. Native bears and opossums were very numerous, as were also kangaroos and wallabies, kangaroo rats and bandicoots. The streams were plentifully stocked with mullet, cat-fish, barramunda and eels. Along the sea-shore the usual produce of the Australian tropical seas was available. Of bird-life there were very many varieties, including large forms like the native companion, the ibis, the forest turkey or bustard, and the emu. The country of the Wakka tribe is more level and open than that of the Kabi. It has little of the bunya and pine scrub.

Not much weight can be attached to the traditions of the natives as to whence they came and by what route. They have been obviously so many generations in their present home, that any reliable tradition regarding where they came from, probably died out thousands of years back. At the same time it ought to be stated that Tindabalu, who was upwards of sixty years of age, and whose father belonged to the country about Gympie, told me that his father had told him, what had been handed down from his ancestors, that their people had come from the north along the coast.

CHAPTER III

WITHOUT measurements, one can only speak approximately regarding stature and other physical characters.

The tribes under notice showed no marked divergence in appearance from the other Queensland blacks or from those whom I have seen belonging to New South Wales, Victoria, and the south of South Australia. It would be impossible to distinguish, by appearance, a Kabi or Wakka black of the darkest complexion from, say, a Victorian black. But there were among the Kabi some with lighter skins than any I have seen in Victoria. Two or three of the women were particularly light in colour. There was a very decided suggestion of a mixture of races. The women seemed of a higher type than those in the west of Victoria and the southern extremity of South Australia. Among these

latter there was a number of bearded women.
I saw some such at Condah settlement and
three at Adelaide, so that to have a beard
must have been a not uncommon feature of
the women of that locality. I have been told
what may be correct, that this peculiarity was
the result of using a razor.

The Kabi and Wakka men were of low
stature. The average would not exceed 5 feet
5 inches. In rare cases a height of about 6
feet was attained. The range would be from
5 feet 1 inch to 6 feet. In proportion to the
men the women were rather tall.

The people were light in the bone. The
lower part of the limbs was usually fine. The
thighs, much more rarely the calves of the legs,
were well developed. The muscles of the back
and breast were often prominent. In walking,
the head was thrown well back. The hair
of the head was luxuriant and wavy, it was
very fine, sometimes glossy, sometimes dull,
and in most cases it appeared black to the
casual observer. Some writers have described
the Australians as having straight hair. Even
Topinard has made this mistake.[1] I doubt

[1] *Anthrop.*, p. 503.

D

whether there was a solitary case of straight hair in the tribes under notice. One or two had yellowish-brown hair. The beard was abundant and the breast was usually hirsute. Two men, Tommy Cain, a Kabi black, and Waruin, whose mother was Kabi and his father Wakka, had hair so pronouncedly curly as to be fitly termed at least frizzy, if not woolly. Strange, the lips of the latter were unusually thick and his nose more negroid than the general cast. His mother had not these peculiarities, so that he apparently inherited them from his Wakka ancestry. Of all the blacks I knew, he was the most good-natured, the best-tempered and the happiest, always smiling and very frequently laughing uproariously. He was indulgent to his wife and very kind to his horse. A peculiar feature was that on one foot he had only four toes.

One boy, Walareyan, was disfigured by a remarkable defect, the arrested development of one arm. It hung from the shoulder like a fleshy wrist, terminating in a finger and a thumb. He was one of twins, the other, a

TOMMY CAIN OF YABBER, MARY RIVER,
QUEENSLAND.

To face p. 74.

TURANDIU, SON OF DICK AND FANNY.

(He was of Class Bonda, Phratry Dilbai, his mother
being a Dhетwaingam and of a light colour.)

To face p. 75.

girl, was put to death by her parents at her birth.

Reference has been made to diversity of complexion. A few were a bronze colour, while the others and notably the short hairy men, were an intensely dark brown. Young children were light in colour but grew darker with age. The blacker the skin the more it was admired, one reason perhaps for the practice which mothers followed of rubbing their new-born infants with a mixture of powdered charcoal and fat.

Two, I knew, had noses much more approximating to the average European form than usual. Dougal, a Yabber boy, who, with a white skin, would easily have passed for a European, and Fanny, the wife of Dick, a woman of splendid physique and carriage, and of a light colour. Half-castes favour most the father's side. Quadroons generally have blue eyes and fair hair. The long upper lip is, perhaps, their most conspicuous aboriginal feature, but some of them could not be distinguished from swarthy European children. I have occasionally seen amongst pure blacks a fairly high and erect forehead, but I have never seen a broad one. Usually it is low and receding. The eye was set deep under shaggy eyebrows, with the white invariably jaundiced. The nose was broad and rather flat but sometimes had a Jewish cast. It was wide at the nostrils, which were open and flexible, dilating freely. In conformity with their idea of beauty, the gins used to press the noses of their infants, especially girls, in order to flatten them. The cheekbones were high, the chin small and retreating, the jaws prognathous, the mouth wide and prominent, the teeth large and white, the lips heavy but not so thick as those of the negro.

The mental faculties of the people were not of a high order. In all matters relating to their own mode of life they showed enough intelligence to promote their individual interests and provide for their limited necessities. But they were unreflective and averse both to abstract reasoning and sustained mental effort. From my knowledge of their capacity, I would consider the mastering of the first book of Euclid an impossibility to the ablest of them.

They were keen observers of Nature in all its phases and also of people's actions. When they were so disposed they were mentally capable of performing any kind of station work, but generally required supervision, otherwise they soon tired and became careless.

In other parts of Australia, particularly on the mission stations in Victoria, numbers of pure blacks have acquired a very fair primary education. I have seen letters, written by a girl trained at the Condah settlement by Rev. J. H. Stähle and Mrs Stähle which, as regards handwriting, style and sentiment, would do credit to any well-educated lady. And I have mentioned, in *Eaglehawk and Crow*,[1] the notable fact, that the aboriginal school at Ramahyuck, in Victoria, stood, for three consecutive years, the highest of all the primary schools in the State in examination results, obtaining *one hundred per cent.* of marks. But I never heard of any member of the Kabi or Wakka tribes, a pure black, acquiring sufficient education to do more than write his name and read short words in simple sentences, both indifferently. Probably they had had little opportunity

[1] *Eag. and Cr.*, p. 78.

to learn.   Yet two attempts had been made to
Christianise and educate the young people of
the Kabi tribe, one at Durundur by the Rev.
D. MacNabb, a representative of the Roman
Catholic Church, the other on Frazer Island by
the Rev. E. Fuller, a Methodist minister.   The
first failed absolutely, the second was, I believe,
far from being a success.   Perhaps different
methods might have succeeded better.

They were very deficient in inventiveness
and in constructive, artistic faculty.   I have
seen some very good sketches made by natives
belonging to other parts of Australia.   But
some specimens of sketching in pencil, which I
have, that were done by Kabi boys, might
have been done equally well with their eyes
shut.

They had a talent for mimicry, were very
fond of fun, and were free from care about the
future.

On the whole, I would say they were a
good-natured, kind and gentle people.   But
their untrained minds were easily disturbed.
When roused to passion they could be very
cruel.   I have been told by white men that
when natives saw a man in a posture in which

he could be easily killed, they felt an impulse to strike a fatal blow, and would warn the man to get up. I can believe that this was true in some cases. They were as a rule very indulgent to children, and just as kind to their dogs. Fathers would sometimes nurse the children and carry a little one straddling on their shoulder.

From the white man's point of view, they were easy-going as regarded both their manners and their morals. There were no regular ablutions, and but little care was taken to ensure that their food should be free from dirt. They had a conscience but it was by no means tender.

No doubt, according to their own code both of manners and morality, they were strict enough. They were fairly truthful and fairly honest in their dealings with the whites. The station boys and the women were usually trust-worthy in the tasks set them, so long as too great a strain was not put upon them. The greatest defect in their character was instability. They were liable to neglect their duty upon pressure and for a paltry consideration. Their want of outlook, their fickleness and weakness of will, are largely the occasion of their giving way so easily to intemperance and other vices.

Of all the aborigines, young and old, known to me personally between 1865 and 1870, only three or four pure blacks and two half-castes were alive in 1906.   The remnants of the Kabi and Wakka tribes are now gathered together, along with blacks from more distant parts, at the Barambah aboriginal reserve. Formerly, every station had a number of aboriginal families, who regarded it as specially their home.   Now there are no camps on the runs, no organised hunts, no corroborees. A feeble old straggler may be occasionally seen alive, clinging to some loved haunt, but the centre of aboriginal life now is at the Government reserve.

The aborigines have no natural incentive to continued, strenuous labour.   They are greatly addicted to gambling and to intoxicating drink when they can procure it.   The men delight to hang idly about the reserve camp, amusing themselves at card-playing and pitch-and-toss. The women as well as the men are given to smoking.   They are very dirty and very indolent. A black gin, lolling about the camp, clad in an ill-fitting, cast-off, tattered gown, begrimed with grease and ashes, is a sad picture of aboriginal degeneracy and parasitism.

A fact that shows out with remarkable prominence is the greater vitality of the half-castes. One half-caste woman, named Jenny Lind, whom I knew as a little girl, has been twice married, and has nine children and thirteen grandchildren all living. The Rev. Geo. Taplin observed a like advantage in vitality in half-castes as compared with pure blacks in South Australia.[1]

The brightest spot at the aboriginal reserve is the school. The children are very tractable and docile. Special features are the quality of their voices and the heartiness of their singing. It is a pity that they, and especially the half-castes, could not be completely rescued from the demoralising influences of camp-life.

The Australian race is doomed to perish rapidly by contact with European civilisation and vice, and, unless there can be secured practically complete detachment from Europeans,

[1] Curr's *Austr. Race*, vol. ii. p. 264.

an experiment that ought to be attempted, no power on earth can prevent its extinction. The pure-bred blacks of the Kabi and Wakka tribes will probably have disappeared within, at most, twenty years.

CHAPTER IV

IT may be mere fancy, but to me the aborigines seemed to harmonise admirably with their surroundings. They were fitted to their country like the kangaroo and the emu, the platypus and the barramunda. Man generally seems to stand outside and above Nature, but they were decidedly a part of it. To see a large squad of them on the march in single file, or bounding along the hillside and shouting in the excitement of the kangaroo hunt, was quite a treat.

When shifting from one camping-ground to another, they usually moved slowly through the bush, the families separating and gathering their food on the way—opossums, bandicoots, honey, grubs, birds, and so forth. At other times they marched along singly, the lords of creation stepping out with elastic tread and graceful bearing, carrying their light weapons with perhaps some game, the weaker vessel loaded with the chattels and possibly a baby on the back in a loop of a rug or sitting stride-leg on a shoulder. Some would carry live firesticks to save the trouble of producing fire by friction. Arrived at the familiar, well-chosen rendezvous, it was the duty of the women to cut the bark for the humpies (dwellings) and prepare the fires.

The ordinary style of house was a mere bark shelter. Three or four sheets of bark were set obliquely with the lower ends in a semicircle, on the ground, and the upper ends, overlapping, gathered together and supported by light saplings. This sufficed for a family. The dwellings were placed a little distance apart, facing in the same direction and each had its own small fire in front. A large fire would have roasted the inmates. Grass was strewn on the floor for a bed. If rain threatened, a rut was dug round the back of the humpy to serve as a drain. The warriors' spears were stuck in the ground, ready to hand, at the side of the rude shelter.

The blacks were astir early, but they could afford to be, as they often slept in the daytime.

In the evening, before retiring, they would squat by the fire or lie awake discoursing, or indulging in a quiet corroboree. On occasions there would be bad blood in the camp, and accusations and retorts would be volubly poured forth in stentorian tones late into the night, followed, perhaps, by the clatter of weapons used in single combat. They were great at invective and wordy strife.

There was much of interest to be observed on visiting a camp. The family could be witnessed at their rather irregular meal. They might be regaling themselves on the eucalyptus - flavoured opossum, the leg of a kangaroo, or the tender, white flesh of a snake. A joint would be placed on the fire, and as it became partially cooked, it would be taken up by the head of the house, who, after helping himself to a few mouthfuls, would be followed by his wife, and then one after another of the children would take a bite in turn, whereupon it would be replaced at the fire. No doubt, eaten in this way the gravy would be delicious, and the adhering ashes would give the zest of salt. Large game, like emus, was cooked in improvised ovens, prepared by scooping a hole in the ground. The operation was nothing like so elaborate as the mode followed in Victoria.

There are two varieties of native bee, both very small. They had no sting and made only a faint hum. One kind, called kĭlla in Kabi, was very dark in colour ; the other kind, known as kavai in Kabi, was a light, greyish colour and its honey was the less esteemed. Their nests were in hollow trees. The natives made a spongy mat out of the inner bark or bast tissue of a tree, by beating and chewing it. This they would dip into honey, which it would absorb like a sponge. The method of use was very sociable and economical. Members of the household would take a suck in turn, and after the substance of the honey was exhausted, the flavour would cling to the bark rag and reward the sucker for his exertions.

The man's chief home duties consisted in cooking and eating. He would also spend much time in fashioning his weapons, using a stone knife or chisel and a shell. The ends of the spears were hardened by fire. Cords were manufactured of fur and of hair, human hair

included. Sinews were drawn from the
kangaroo's tail to serve as twine. They were
used for sewing opossums' skins together to
form rugs. Much time was spent in preparing
the rugs. The flesh was rubbed off the skins
with stones. Generally a rude linear design
was scratched on the inside of each skin and
coloured with *kuthing*, a red clay. The women
were skilled in the manufacture of nets and of
dillie-bags made of grass or twine.

When other occupations failed, they could
always entertain themselves profitably searching one another's heads. When engaged in
this way they put one very much in mind of
monkeys.

The men might go out for the chase either in
a band or singly, They used to fire the grass
in a line from one projecting point of scrub to
another and force the game away to a corner,
formed by the scrub margin, where their
comrades would be lying in wait to effect the
slaughter. At other times, just by loud shouting, they would confuse the mobs of marsupials,
while they would be following them up, running
with a long stride, and prepared to strike with
spear or waddy as chance offered. It stirred

the onlooker's blood to see them, in a state of
nature, running and leaping through the bush,
as wild-like as the creatures they were pursuing, and to hear their hunting halloes rever-
berating in the virgin forest.

It must have been painfully slow work,
cutting an opossum out of a hollow tree with
the stone axe.   It was less laboriously employed
for stripping the bark of trees and for cutting
notches for the toes to assist in climbing.   The
climbing vine was in constant use.   It was cut
long enough to compass the thickest trees and
the user's body with a few feet to spare.   A
loose open knot was formed at one end, so as
to afford a good hold for the left hand.   By
passing the other end round his back and
holding it in the same hand, the climber could
lean back on the vine and have his right hand
free for using the tomahawk.   Those dexterous
in the use of the *yuru*, could walk quickly up
the smooth stem of a tree to any height.   The
tomahawk, when not required to cut notches,
would be held on the front of the shoulder by
the pressure of the jaw, or would be stuck in
the girdle.

In the territory of the Kabi and Wakka, as

we have seen, food was plentiful and in great variety. The animal food embraced almost every living thing from a fly to a man. The presence of large grubs, called *buruga*, in living trees, was detected by the wood-dust they dislodged, which could easily be seen on the ground or at the entrance of the hole they had made. If the grub was far in, an incision was made in the tree, and it was picked out with a pointed stick. They ate the grub, either raw or roasted, rejecting the head. These grubs are a delicate food. They have the flavour and consistency of a soft, rice pudding, enriched with eggs. I speak from experience, having eaten them repeatedly. The natives were very expert in catching animals, knowing exactly how to get hold of them so as to prevent injury to themselves. Fresh-water turtles were captured very neatly. The black would swim very quietly till he got near where the creature's nose was visible above water. When approaching still closer, he would tread water, slip his hand under the unsuspecting turtle, and catch it without any difficulty. The eggs of the turtle, found in their holes in the bank, were also eaten.

E

All kinds of marsupials were eaten. The flesh of the kangaroo has very much the same flavour as beef. Opossums have a rather objectionable taste of their staple food, the gum-tree leaf. The bandicoot, a small marsupial, is very plump, and when roasted on the coals, as tasty as sucking-pig. Snake flesh is very white and tender in appearance. All lizards were eaten. The iguana has an oily, fishy taste. The same remark applies to its eggs, which are deposited in a string in disused ant-hills.

Birds of all sorts were counted good eating. The scrub-turkey, or wawoon, was a great favourite. Its eggs, laid in a large mound formed of soft soil and withered leaves, were as large and as palatable as those of the domestic turkey. The boomerang was used for killing ducks.

Fish were speared and also caught with a small hand-net fixed at the end of two pieces of wood, which were held by the other ends. Eels were also an article of diet.

While all these kinds of animal food mentioned, as well as many other kinds, not necessary to be mentioned here, were eaten generally by some, certain animals and other kinds of food as well, were forbidden to the young, and at times to women. Thus, eels were forbidden to children. They were warned that if they ate them their nose would become cancerous. I knew a man whose nose was partly eaten away by gangrene, and the cause was said to be that he had indulged in eels. The young were not only prohibited from eating emu eggs, they were not even allowed to look at them. Infringement of this rule, it was believed, would be followed by pimples breaking out on the nose. One season, the women told me that bunyas were *mundha* (tapu), to them, and they begged for mutton. Other kinds of food proscribed to minors on pain of disease or sickness were, porcupine, snakes, fresh-water fish, kangaroo hurt, scrub - turkey eggs, and the flying fox.

Of vegetable food there was not much variety. Miss Petrie has given an account of what was used by the Brisbane blacks, which applies, I believe, in every particular, to the tribes here treated of. She also gives a list of the botanical names, which I shall not repeat.

Yams, fern-roots, the roots of the *cunjevoi*, the core of the top of the cabbage-palm, and a few wild fruits, such as the quandong, the native plum, and the native lime, were the most common. It was the recognised duty of the women to dig the yams (*Dioscorea Transversa*) for family use. They were regularly provided with the yam-stick for this purpose, a staff about five feet long, the thickness of a stout walking-stick, and pointed at both ends. It served another purpose equally well, being the women's fighting weapon. They used it like a single-stick with great deftness in their feminine encounters. The *cunjevoi* (*Alocasia Macrorhiza*) grew luxuriantly in the Kabi country, about the beds of the creeks. It has a large, broad, glossy leaf, with stalks set close together in a big bunch, and closely resembles the Arum lily. The juice, being poisonous, had to be expressed from the roots, which were then roasted before being eaten.

But, for the Kabi people especially, the most esteemed vegetable food was the product of the beautiful bunya tree (*Araucaria Bidwillii*). The top towers aloft like a graceful dome above the surrounding foliage of the scrub. So far as my experience went, it seemed to bear annually, but it is said to be most prolific every third year. The cone sometimes attains a great size, the maximum diameters being as large as 16 in. by 9 in. The seeds are an inch to an inch and a half long and half an inch thick at the thicker end. Their tissue is like that of a potato. When the seed is young, it is juicy and soft and it is eaten entire and raw. As it matures the embryo assumes a more definite form and is rejected ; the surrounding tissue, at the same time, becomes drier and less palatable. When mature, the seed is preferred roasted. Before being roasted, each seed is partially bruised with a stone. When it has been in the fire for a minute or two it gives a crack, the signal that it is cooked. They sometimes pounded the roasted seed into a kind of meal, which they called *nyangu*. They showed exceptional foresight in laying up a store of bunyas. They picked the seeds out of the cone, leaving untouched the tough envelope with which they are covered, then they put them into netted bags and buried them about the beds of the creeks to be ready for future consumption. Bunyas thus stored came to have a very offensive smell, which they imparted to all that came into contact with them. Still the blacks ate them with great relish, although they made their breath smell much worse than if they had eaten raw onions. The ripe seeds have a resinous flavour when roasted, which is more decided when they are boiled. The best evidence of their value as a nutritious food was the way the natives throve upon them. In the bunya season they became visibly fat. Certain trees were claimed by individuals. The local blacks were proud of their bunya tree and very fond of the fruit. At the prospect of an abundant yield, tribes would gather from a distance of upwards of a hundred miles to feast upon the bunya. The visit usually terminated with a battle.

Cannibalism had been practised, but after the prejudices of the whites became known, it was very rarely indulged in. Apparently, human beings were not killed for the express purpose of being eaten, but portions of deceased persons not emaciated, and the flesh of those killed in fighting, were consumed as food. Individuals were unwilling to own to cannibalism themselves, but would admit that others were given to it.

When not moving among the white people, the natives were content with Nature's livery for clothing and were not ashamed. The opossum rug was worn like a shawl about the shoulders in cold weather and formed a covering at night. The papery bark of the tea tree (*nambur nambur*) had at a former time been similarly used. Other clothing they had none, but they adorned themselves with a few ornaments. Their girdle, made of hair-twine or other cord, was a convenient receptacle for the tomahawk or other implement. The head-band, also of plaited cord, or of the skin of the dingo's tail, was more for adornment than utility. I have seen those made of cord coloured with pipeclay. On special occasions white feathers would be stuck in front. Both sexes would wear a piece of mother-of-pearl shell suspended by a string from the neck; this was known as a *dulin*.

Another kind of *dulin* worn by the women was a piece of native dogskin cut off the posterior. The women wore long necklaces of beads made of a yellow reed, and the men had the septum of the nose perforated to hold a thin piece of bone or wood.

CHAPTER V

THE practices of circumcision and subincision were, in my opinion, introduced into Australia from the north-west in comparatively recent times. They spread over Central Australia, but did not reach the south-west of West Australia nor Victoria, and they affected New South Wales only on the north-west corner and Queensland on the western boundary. These rites were unknown among the Kabi and Wakka and surrounding tribes. The other ceremonies attending initiation to manhood were, with local variations, common to the whole of Australia. If they had not been so long disused in the settled districts, the details there would probably not differ very much from those so minutely described by Spencer and Gillen as characterising initiation in Central Australia.

Two words were employed by the Kabi to

designate the man-making ceremonies, viz., Dhur (a circle) and Kīvar-yĕngga (man-making). I am not aware of initiation on a grand scale having taken place after 1865, the date of my first acquaintance with the natives. In former years, special places for conducting the ceremonies were selected, on which various tribes would converge, in order that they might all participate by contributing candidates and assisting in the performances. Places specially named to me were Boobangery on the Yabber run, Waraba near Caboolture, and Biuoraba near Ipswich. I shall endeavour to fuse together several accounts, in which the sequence of events is uncertain.

Certain individuals, called Kamaran, *i.e.*, headmen, qualified by their experience, were appointed to conduct the proceedings. The various tribes camped apart and the initiation of the youth of one tribe was superintended by Kamaran of another. An essential requisite was a large circle, or Dhur, which, as was done elsewhere, would be formed by a low bank of earth. The proceedings, which, according to one account, covered about a month, begin by the youths having to spend a night camped within the circle. They have no fire but are allowed rugs of kangaroo skin. In the morning they are taken out of the ring, each in charge of Kamaran, who watch them and direct their movements.

The women are camping apart from the men and no intercourse is permitted between them and the novitiates. The latter frequently repeat a spell—" Ngudha, ngudha, ngudha, ngudha, mīnya, mīnya, ka!" As my informant did not know the meaning of these words, I conclude that they were either corrupt or borrowed from another dialect, or else so archaic that their meaning had been forgotten.

On the first day the older men hold a grand corroboree.

While being conducted by the Kamaran, if a snake is met with, the Bŏndaban (bull-roarer) is whirled, the snake is killed and shown to the youths, but they are not allowed to partake of it. In fact, fasting is part of the ordeal. In the evening, samples of mundha (prohibited food) are handed round among them for inspection. Their hunger is appeased surreptitiously by portions of opossum being given to them without the knowledge of the Kamaran. The concealment is probably fictitious. At this juncture a rug is wrapped about the head to hide the youth from the old men, just as mother-in-law and son-in-law cover the head at times to avoid seeing each other. The boys are prohibited from looking up at the sky.

On the second day they are washed and the hair is shaved off all parts of the body but the head. In some parts of Australia the hair is plucked out, and probably this would be the primitive practice with the Kabi, Wakka and adjoining tribes.

Various fire ceremonies are performed, corresponding to the Engwura of the Arunta. In one of these, the young men join hands and march round a fire, the young women simultaneously doing the same at another fire.

All levity is forbidden on penalty of severe punishment. One informant said that laughter was liable to be punished with death. A sorcerer would kill the delinquent with a Kundīr (crystal.) And yet the Kamaran had recourse to ridiculous antics to test the power of the young men to maintain their gravity. The other extreme was also followed in order to try them and discipline them. Various means were employed to make them afraid. A hole was made in the ground. One of the old men went into it and represented various animals, such as the emu and the kangaroo. This was probably a totemic representation. A sham fight was another means resorted to for terrifying the boys.

Each boy is now allotted a separate camp, prepared for him by two blacks, one of whom remains with him. He sleeps there one night. The next morning the novitiates, who are painted red, are taken out into the bush and at sunset are brought near to the main camp. As the sun goes down, a gin, who is also painted red, begins to sing so that the boys can hear her. The following is one of the songs sung on these occasions :—

> Kung bŏndyin'-dimān
> Water shake
>
> Ngan'-daigaru'   dŏm'-an dŏmān'   buthān'
> The mullet-with little little   close to.
>   Bur'-un burūn', tang'-gara kak'-kalīm',
>   A fish, a fish, the mouth gleaming,

Windan'	windan'	buthān',
The bank,	the bank	close to,
Tang'-gara	kak'-kalim'.	
The mouth	gleaming.	

When the boys hear the singing, they draw near the camp in a string, but are not yet allowed to enter it. They have now to camp together. To this common camp they retire, and with their attendants, march round it four times. Before daylight they are taken out from their camp again and at sundown brought near the main camp, when the same gin repeats her singing.

About a score of fires are now made in a line and are covered with green leaves to produce a dense smoke. Beginning at that end of the row of fires which is farthest from the women's camp, the novitiates jump into the first fire, clapping their hands, and repeat the jumping and hand-clapping at every fire till they come to the last, which is close to the camp of the women, and there they stay the night.

Next day the boys are once more taken out into the bush, each in care of two Kamaran. Some of the old men remain behind and prepare an immense fire. At night the boys are made to jump upon the red-hot embers until they are extinguished.

After this fire ceremony, there comes, upon the sixth day, the naming ceremony, called Wamaran, which is carried out like a sort of roll-call. Three large fires are made, round one or other of which all the blacks are congregated. The youths with one attendant are at one of the fires, the other attendants, sharing in the duties of initiation, are at another. These call out to each boy in turn a name that has been selected for him, obviously an additional name to the one he received at birth. The boy, as he receives his name, responds, "Kai ngai" ("Here am I"). Each is then asked if he would like to have a wife, and an affirmative answer is given. At night, the married women take charge of the young men, the married men camping apart. According to one account, this ends the initiation.

Another account, which represents the institution as protracted for a month, adds subsequent proceedings, as follows :—Efforts are continued to provoke both laughter and fear. But the boys have been forewarned by one of the old men what to expect, and advised how to behave, so that they may dare to throw stones at those trying to make them laugh.

Afterwards the boys are put out of the camp, and while being chased by one party of seniors are met by another, who catch them and toss them up, letting them fall down upon the ground.

Following upon the tossing, the elders perform a corroboree for the delectation of the novitiates. Each youth, with his head covered up, is then carried upon the shoulders of one of the initiators, who cries out: "There's a big flood, we must cross the creek." This of course is only make-believe, but the boy is led to suppose he has run the risk of drowning.

They are taken back to the camp, and, when let go, another party of men approaches, ready for fighting. One of them gives two cooeys and immediately the young fellows begin to paint their helemon (shields), preparing for battle. But, before starting, they give one united cooey. They are then associated with one party of men, preparatory to engaging in real fighting, and the following day a fight takes place in earnest. When the fight is over, all the gins, both young and old, welcome the youths to the camp, clapping on the front of their thighs with their hands placed both together.

The young men are next taken into the large circle, and, amid much shouting, singing and yelling, one of the wizards cuts them on the shoulder or back with a crystal, to form cicatrices distinctive of the tribe the particular boy belongs to. One account affirms that other attendants also cut the boy on the back and chest, and that after considerable howling, the boys are taken out of the circle back to their camp.

When the incisions are healed, the novitiate enters the common camp, where, at first, no notice is taken of him. He has his own sleeping place, which he must not leave, and where a gin must not as yet venture. What appears to be a marriage ceremony now occurs. A gin painted red, and having a cockatoo feather in her hair, is brought to the boy by one of the Kamaran, who pulls the feather out of

F

her hair and places it on the hair of the boy.
The gin may then return to her own camp
without even touching him.   When taken back
to the camp by the old man, all the other
females salute her, clapping their hands on
their thighs as already described.   For about
a week the young man is not allowed to look
in the direction of the women's camp.   Then
the young gin returns and makes a camp by
him.   They touch each other and thereby they
become man and wife.

No doubt the foregoing accounts combined
of the initiation ceremonies are at best fragmentary, but they embody all that was
essential, and the marriage ceremony as
described above is a fresh and unique
feature.

The bodies of the men were invariably
ornamented with gaping cicatrices.   The
different tribes were distinguished by the
patterns according to which the scars were
arranged.   They were cut on the muscular
parts of the back, breast, and upper arm with
a crystal, a shell, or a sharp flint.   After a
deep incision had been made, the wound was
filled up with a paste of fat and powdered char-

coal, to keep it open. It sloughed for some time and, when healed, had the appearance of two lips. The formation of certain cicatrices, as has been seen, constituted a painful part of the initiation ceremonies, but others were incised under much milder conditions. I once witnessed three or four being cut on a youth of about twenty years of age by his own mother, evidently at his own request. He was lying on the ground face down, while she was carving away at his back with a piece of glass.

Besides the incisions made for adornment, others were made as an expression of grief. In this matter the women exceeded the men. After a night of mourning, I have seen their bodies marked with small incisions from top to toe, with the dry blood still about them. The women incised the front of the head for grief, the men the back of the head. Occasionally they paid respect to the memory of white people in the same way. My uncle, Mr John Mortimer, had stood by a blackfellow, Buyu Marom (Calves Fat), who was tried for murder. This black was really innocent, and being acquitted, he ever afterward cherished a grateful regard for my uncle, and when he heard of his death, he showed his sorrow by inflicting a deep wound with his tomahawk on his own head.

Another practice of personal adornment, followed by most of the men, was the piercing of the septum of the nose. A piece of bone or wood was inserted in the hole and thus worn when the man was in full dress. After contact with civilisation, the perforation occasionally served as a convenient receptacle for holding a tobacco pipe.

Among the Bīdhala, or coast blacks, there were certain practices in vogue which were not observed by the Wapa, or inland blacks. The women of the Bīdhala, in some places, had one of the front teeth purposely knocked out. In other parts of Australia this mutilation was performed on the young men.

The Bīdhala females, in childhood, had also the point of the little finger of the left hand removed at the first joint. The process was very simple and probably painless. A slender string made of the strong web of a spider was wound tightly round the joint. By this means the circulation of the blood was effectually stopped, and the point of the finger ultimately dropped off. A similar practice prevailed at the Daly River, not far from Port Darwin in the Northern Territory.

CHAPTER VI

DISEASE AND TREATMENT, DEATH, BURIAL
AND MOURNING

BEFORE they became tainted with diseases
contracted from Europeans, the aborigines
were a healthy and hardy race. Their out-
door life and the necessary struggle for existence kept them toned up physically. No
epidemics are known to have occurred. Their
maladies were such as would arise from accident, exposure, strain and errors of diet.
Indigestion, rheumatism and toothache were
common troubles. Leprosy was unknown, but
I knew the case of a man whose nose was in
a state of chronic gangrene. Heart disease,
probably the result of strain, judging from
cases I witnessed, would not be rare. The
partial adoption of European habits both
aggravated the maladies they were naturally
liable to and induced others of a more serious
nature, such as syphilis and phthisis. Since

contact with white people, the great majority of deaths has been the result of phthisis, and this scourge has been specially fatal to the young.

In their pristine condition the natives seemed to have lived to an old age. I knew a few people of seventy years and upwards. One woman, who used to be carried about from camp to camp, had become wizened like a mummy.

Their medical skill was very limited, for the most part mere illusion, and of surgical skill they had virtually none. To allay pain they would apply a tight bandage, and sores they would cover over with clay or ashes. Ligatures were fastened above boils or wounds on the limbs, to give relief by checking the circulation. A favourite treatment of local pain was for the Manngur (wizard) to suck the part if accessible to his mouth. The sucking would of itself relieve inflammation and the doctor would increase the relief by a mild deception. A friend of mine saw one treating a sore part by suction and expectorating blood, which was supposed to be drawn from the affected part in the patient. But as a matter of fact, the doctor showed my friend a kundīr (quartz crystal), with which he had been lacerating his own gums while performing the operation, so that it was a case of bleeding by proxy.

I once saw a similar but more elaborate process of bleeding. A boy, complaining of a pain in the stomach, had one end of a cord fastened about the abdomen. The other end was immersed in a vessel with water. The Manngur held the cord near the middle by both hands, see-sawing it across his gums, and from time to time expectorating into the vessel. This was supposed to be a bleeding of the patient. It was carried on with much patience and seriousness, and as medicine to be efficacious must needs be nasty, when the operation is over, the boy drinks the potion in the vessel. I was scowled at for regarding the operation with amused credulity.

Sickness, not the obvious result of accident, was always attributed to sorcery. The ordinary belief of the blackfellow who had mysteriously become sick was that some enemy, from a place of concealment, had launched a magic stone at him, which had become embedded in his body. It was the business of the sorcerer, by his hocus-pocus tricks, to extract the stone or whatever other foreign body was causing the pain. As if on the principle that like cures like, a magic stone was sometimes applied to the affected part to allay the pain. The stones known as kundīr and minkŏm, when imagined to be residing in the sorcerer's own body, were assumed causes of exceptional vitality, but they could be utilised by him as lethal weapons.

Ginggil ginggil, a kind of mange contracted from the dogs, was very prevalent. The only treatment applied was pressing the pimples of the rash with a dull-pointed stick a few inches in length. This operation seemed to be much enjoyed—at least it was often practised, and was carried out with apparent zest, the body being picked all over very methodically.

After death there was usually a cannibal feast, and profound mourning was invariably engaged in nightly by the whole camp and prolonged for several weeks. The skin was sometimes taken off, and parts like the knee-caps and the toes were also removed. Bones of the arms, legs and head would be fractured to obtain pieces convenient for carrying. These relics would be treasured by relatives for five or six years. The women would carry them about with them and would store them in the cosiest corner of the camp.

There were different methods of disposing of the dead. One mode was to erect a stage for the body on a tree, or to construct one of saplings and bark resting on upright forks. On such stages the body was left until completely desiccated, when the bones would be deposited in a hollow tree. After contact with Europeans the common method was interment in the ground. One grave I knew was marked by small logs being carefully arranged on the surface, which were said to represent the brothers of the deceased, and the position of the logs was intended to point out where they lived.

The young folk were prohibited from partaking of human flesh. The distinction as to who should partake, would suggest that other motives than the mere appeasing of appetite conduced to uphold cannibalism.

A strip of skin taken from the thigh was sometimes wrapped round a spear and employed as a magical indicator to discover the person who had by sorcery or other cause, been the agent of death.

The duration of mourning was about six weeks. At night mourners could be seen flitting about the camp carrying glowing torches, for the purpose, it was said, of driving off the spirits. I have seen the gleam of the torches, but as the explanation of their use was given me by whites it may not be reliable.

Every night a general, loud wailing was sustained for hours, and was accompanied by personal laceration with sharp flints or other cutting instruments. The men would be content with a few incisions on the back of the head, but the women would gash themselves from head to foot and allow the blood to dry upon the skin.

The cry of the mourners was :—

> " Ngata ! ngata ! mĭmin ! mĭmin !
> Wuthung nganyunggai balomathi gindī !"
> " Brother   my   is dead   oh dear !"

The meaning of the first four words was unknown to my informant. After this wail there would follow a long-drawn ululation.

To join with others in mourning for their friends was considered a sympathetic, courteous and proper action. A blackfellow, once complaining to me about the unkindness of another, regarded it as all the more reprehensible, seeing that he had joined in the mourning for the ungrateful man's brother.

As a sign of mourning the women tied bunches of emu feathers in their hair all over the head, and these were left to drop off gradually in course of time. During mourning certain kinds of food had to be avoided as mundha (tapu). Fasting for the dead was called ngarīn. The names of the dead were not uttered. They were usually referred to as kananngur, *i.e.*, poor fellow.

CHAPTER VII

ART, IMPLEMENTS, UTENSILS, WEAPONS, CORROBOREES

THE tribes of Central and North - Central
Australia, having been recently minutely described in all the uncanny, uncouth, and
picturesque details of unsophisticated savage
life, there is a liability to imagine that they
represent the most primitive phase of Australian aboriginal culture. But in many
respects they are more highly advanced than
those tribes with which we have been long
familiar, who occupy, or have occupied, the
early settled districts. The territory of the
central tribes is very extensive, and is easily
accessible to influence from the north, the
direction from which advances in Australia
have always come. The distribution of circumcision is one evidence of greater accessi-
bility to foreign influence and, besides, art, as
exhibited in weapons, ornaments and imple-

ments, is much more highly developed in the
north and centre of Australia than along the
east coast. The rivers emptying into the
Pacific and Indian Oceans have formed barriers
to intercourse, whereas, on the contrary, rivers
flowing into the Gulf of Carpentaria have been
like highways leading inwards, and the ranges
running east and west once crossed, numerous
other water-courses, which converge upon the
very heart of the continent, have facilitated the
introduction of higher culture.

The tribes under notice, like most tribes on
the east coast, were kept to a large extent
isolated by river and mountain barriers.
Several facts indicate their peculiar primitive-
ness. The wommera for spear-throwing was
not in use. The spears were without stone
tips ; they had no prongs apart from the shaft
itself. The only barb they had was cut out of
the solid, and this was rare. There was little
or no carving on their weapons for ornament,
and any coloured designs were of the simplest
outline. Besides, their manufactured articles
of any kind were comparatively few.

As regards implements the muyīm, or stone-
axe, was the most useful and important. Of

the axes there were different makes. They were chipped and ground to an edge. I have two in my possession, both of diorite. One is 4½ in. long, 1¼ in. thick, and when in its perfect state must have been nearly as broad as long. Without a handle, it weighs 15½ ozs. The other is 6¾ in. long, 4 in. broad, 2½ in. in greatest thickness, and 2½ lbs. in weight. The handles were formed of pieces of the scrub-vine or a withy doubled round the middle of the stone, secured with grass-tree gum, and the ends forming the haft held together by being wrapped round tightly with cord. Another make was unique in shape, and was known by the name of waggara. A specimen is to be seen in the Brisbane Museum. The head is cylindrical, about 2 in. thick and 4½ in. in length. The cutting end is bevelled like a wedge, the other end is rounded for use as a hammer. The handle is wrapped round with emu-skin, having the feathers on.

Stone knives, known simply as dhakkē (a stone), were also in use. They were made of quartzite. One, that I have, is very broad, the edge having a large curve. It shows marks of having been flaked with a straight-edged stone, which must have been used as a chisel and struck with, probably, a piece of wood. It may have had a handle, but could have been used without one for flaying and dissecting game.

Flints and shells were also used as knives, and served as spokeshaves and chisels for dressing weapons. Bone awls were employed to assist in sewing. String was made of kangaroo sinews, the fur of the squirrel and human hair. The inner bark of trees, such as the currajong and stringy-bark, was also utilised as cordage.

Before the tinder-box was obtained from Europeans, fire was produced by friction, the flower-stalks of the grass tree (Xanthorrhœa) being employed for the purpose. One stalk was laid horizontally on the ground. Into a notch in it, the end of a lighter stem, held vertically, was inserted. This latter was then twirled rapidly round, backwards and forwards, between the two hands until ignition took place. Round about the notch there was placed some dry bark, rubbed soft, which easily caught fire and could be blown into a flame.

The yuru, or climbing-vine (*Flagellaria*

A NATIVE OF THE KABI TRIBE, MARYBOROUGH, QUEENSLAND.

To face p. 121.

Indica), was of very great service and a regular article of the family kit. Both men and women were expert in the use of it, which has been already described.

The construction of bark canoes was understood, but they were rarely called into requisition.

Utensils were few. The coolaman, or wooden basin for holding water, had been superseded by the tin can for general use before I became acquainted with the natives. They employed stones for grinding the bunya-nuts into meal. The women made dillie - bags of various patterns and sizes, the material being grass or string of squirrel fur. Small hand-nets were also manufactured.

Their weapons were of few and simple varieties. The kuthar, usually called nulla-nulla by Europeans, was used as a club either to be thrown or for striking at close quarters. With it they both hunted and fought. The heavy end was sometimes rendered more formidable by having a surrounding band of knobs carved in the solid. The kuthar were commonly made of iron-bark, but many were of brigalow, and specimens of the scented myal,

G

obtained from a distance by barter, were very
highly prized.

The boomerangs were narrow, light and
devoid of ornamental carvings. Some returned
to the thrower, others only sped forward. The
blacks could not distinguish the one sort from
the other by inspection, but only upon trial.

A weapon called *bŏkkan*, from *bŏkka*, a horn
or projection, corresponded to the leangil of
the Victorians. It was rectangular in outline,
the striking end pointed and shorter than the
handle, and it was wielded like a light pick-
axe.

The spears, or kŏni, were from 7 to 10 ft.
in length, made of iron-bark saplings and
hardened at the point by the application of
fire. They were usually quite plain, but occasionally had a single barb. They were cast
without the help of the lever or throwing-
stick.

The shields were only of one pattern, oblong
in shape, with ends rounded, and about 2 ft.
long by 1 ft. wide. They were sometimes called helemon, a word borrowed from
the New South Wales dialects, but the local
name was kunmarim, after the currajong tree,

from the wood of which they were formed. They had to be thick to allow of a handle being made at the back by cutting and burning a hollow under a short longitudinal bar. Although very light the wood was exceedingly tough. Some old ones showed many deep dents and prints from blows received, and yet they were sound. The front was generally coloured with red and white pigment by way of ornamentation.

In prehistoric times stone knives had been utilised for hand-to-hand single combats, the combatants each clasping each other with one arm and striking the knife into the thigh or a fleshy part of the back until one cried "Hold." Pieces of butcher knives, hafted after the style of the old stone knives, came to be used for the same manner of fighting and inflicted frightful gashes. A boy Donald received a terrible, deep wound in his thigh in this way, which festered, kept him lying in the camp for weeks, and rendered him lame for long afterwards.

In their regular warfare the spear was the offensive weapon. The warriors advanced to meet each other in two extended lines and they fought two and two, *i.e.*, a man on one side engaged one on the other.

The message-stick in use was of a very simple form. It was merely a tiny bit of a twig bearing a few notches by way of inscription. On one occasion, when we were resuming our journey after passing the night at Gigoomgan, my blackboy produced a piece of a stick, $1\frac{1}{2}$ in. in length, out of the lining of his hat and showed it to me. It had three small notches on one side. He explained that this was a love-letter, that the notch in the middle represented him the Dhŏmka, or messenger, and those on either side, the young man sending the message and the girl for whom it was intended respectively. The two had met at the bunya season some time previous, and the lover was renewing his vows by this means. The letter had to be carried in the hat for a month or two before he had an opportunity of delivering it.

The corroboree was a very essential element in the occupation and pastimes of the natives. In its elaborate forms for public performance, it combined the play, the song and the dance. The composer of a new corroboree was re-

NATIVES OF YABBER, KABI TRIBE, MARY RIVER, QUEENSLAND.

garded as a person of consequence. He instructed the performers and led off in the representations before both his own tribe and its neighbours. The music was generally a rather monotonous chant, often rising suddenly an octave while preserving the same melody. The grand corroborees were given at night, the stage being a level plot of ground illumined by fires. The performers were painted fantastically with red and white clay, and sometimes decorated with feathers. They were usually disposed in ranks, and advanced from the background towards the fires. Part of the dancing motion was a peculiar quivering of the legs, the feet being spread apart. This peculiarity seems to have been common throughout Australia.

The women assisted as a kind of orchestra, sitting in front and clapping with their hands upon stretched opossum skin or on their own thighs.

There was often a little plot in the corroboree, the machinery being always very simple. On Bonara station, I once saw a structure, like a rude flat-roofed house, made of strong uprights with forks at the upper end.

On these there was arranged a kind of floor or scaffolding of saplings and boughs. I was told by my black companion that the men performed on the raised stage, and at a time appointed rushed down among the women, who were congregated below, and behaved licentiously.

At Monsildale, a tributary of the Brisbane, there was a carved log intended to represent an eaglehawk. It formed part of the accessories of what was known as the Eaglehawk Corroboree, which had been transmitted from some place distant and unknown. One of the interesting facts about corroborees was that they travelled great distances, and were repeated by tribes to whom the words of them were unintelligible.

The corroborees, composed to be rendered in public on a large scale, with dancing and other accompaniments, were often sung in private to while away the hour, the singers keeping time by striking a pair of boomerangs or nulla-nullas together.

The natives had their canons of taste as regards singing. I have heard them take off one another very well in the matter

of tremolo and other faults of tone pro-
duction.

The one theme would be varied from andante
to allegro. A common signal for a change of
time or melody was to trill one sustained note
to the sound of the letter *r.* This answered
the purpose of the ringing of a bell.

Popular English songs were transformed
into corroborees and sung lustily by a group of
blackboys, after corroboree style, without their
comprehending the sense.

The blacks were all given to the composi-
tion of little ditties or lyrics on passing events,
efforts in occasional verse, as they might be
called. Sometimes they mixed up the English
and aboriginal languages with a ludicrous
effect.

CHAPTER VIII

SOCIAL ORGANISATION

THE term tribe as applied to the aborigines is somewhat vague. It has no reference to numbers, or extent of territory, or political unity. The bond of tribal affinity, that has generally been recognised, is community of language. This is invariably the strongest bond, and involves and implies other factors making for union. There was no chieftain, no organised government. There are no chiefs, in the ordinary application of the word, in Australia. A few families claiming the same territory usually camped and travelled together, sometimes in smaller, sometimes in larger numbers. I characterise such family groups as communities. Dr Howitt's Kaiabara was merely a group like this and not a tribe. He locates it at Widgee, whereas the name I got for the Widgee people was Gīgarbŏra. On his map its locality is placed near the Boyne

River, in the Wakka country, where it could not possibly have its home. Its habitat was probably somewhere a little to the south of Widgee. Communities designated by some feature distinguishing either themselves or their country, the term for which was prefixed to the termination -bŏra, were, apparently, more numerous among the Kabi people than in any other tribe. But such communities were constituted by a few families occupying the same small area in common.

The older men, and especially those of conspicuous courage and force of character, laid down the hereditary law and saw it enforced. The bond of speech is exemplified by the fact that along the greater part of the east of Australia the tribes are distinguished from one another by their respective negatives.

The list of the communities whose names I have received, with the meaning of the stem so far as known, and the approximate habitat, is as follows :—

Community	*Meaning*	*Locality*
Wutyabŏra	wutya, cedar	Kilkivan
Buabŏra or	bua, foul smell	
Bugabŏra		

Community	Meaning	Locality
Kaiyabŏra	kaiya, bite	near Widgee
Wanggurbŏra		
Kinayinbŏra		
Kunambŏra	kunyam, pine tree	
Jakālinbŏra		
Gundabŏra	gunda, cabbage tree	S. of Mt. Boppel
Wityinbŏra		Maryborough
Dauwabŏra	dauwa, noise of hacking	N. of Mt. Boppel
Gīgarbŏra	gīgar, sweet	Widgee
Butyinbŏra		Musket Flat
Baiyambŏra	paiyum, a pipe?	Yabber
Kulībŏra	kulī, native bees' wax	near Barambah
Patyala	, emphatic speaking	Frazer Island
Magumbŏra	magum, edible root in swamp	Eureka

Only two or three of the above were given to Dr Howitt by his informants, but his list contains a number of additional names.

The termination -bŏra, probably means folk, and may correspond to Nambarra, a Cape York word, and Wimbaja, a Darling word, with a like meaning. A personal adjective is formed from these community names by adding -mana. Thus a man would be said to be

Kulĭbŏramana, *i.e.*, he belonged to the Kulĭbŏra. The termination -gan, was added after -bŏra to designate a female of the community.

The classes, which restricted and regulated marriage, in the Kabi, Wakka, Gurang and neighbouring tribes, were four in number. On the system of these tribes and their neighbours, Dr Howitt is confused and misleading. He appears to have obtained inaccurate information from his earliest informant. Relying upon the erroneous information, he came to the conclusion that these tribes reckoned descent through the father. His map shows this district as having patrilineal descent, and Mr N. W. Thomas[1] has accepted his conclusions as correct. In Curr's *Australian Race*, 1886 (vol. iii. pp. 162-163), I gave a correct but incomplete account of the system. I repeated it, with additional details, in my paper in the *Proceedings of the Roy. Soc. of N.S.W.*, in 1889, pp. 402-403, where I say : "There is this peculiarity about the descent, which is, perhaps, also a proof that the four classes are sub-divisions of a primary two, that the class-name alternates from mother to off-

[1] *Kin. and Mar.*, pp. 17, 40; map, p. 43.

spring by a continual recurrence of the same pair of names, thus one line of descent will be Barang, Balkun, and the other Bŏnda, Dhĕrwen *ad infinitum.*" Again, in *Eaglehawk and Crow*, 1899, p. 99, I gave a correct account of the system and re-affirmed the matrilineal descent. But in spite of all this, Dr Howitt, in his *Native Tribes of South-East Australia*, 1904, p. 116 *et seq.*, persisted in his error. The account given by Mr R. H. Mathews is in harmony with mine.[1]

I shall now give a full account of the Kabi and Wakka systems, and show with clearness and absolute certainty that Dr Howitt, usually so accurate, has misapprehended them, and, inferentially, the neighbouring systems, with corresponding classes.

The class-names in Kabi and Wakka, with the corresponding ones considerably to the west and extending far to the north, were as follows :—

Kabi	Wakka	To West and North
Balkuin	Banjur	Kuburu
Barang	Barang	Wun-gu
Dhĕrwain	Choroin	Kurgilu
Bŏnda	Bŏnda	Bŏnbŏri

[1] *R. G. S. of Austr. Q.*, pp. 84-86.

The Gurang Gurang, immediately to the north of the Wakka, the Tarmbal on the Dawson, the Turubul on the Brisbane, the Goenpul on Stradbroke Island,[1] the Kittabool, at the sources of the Clarence, Richmond and Logan Rivers,[2] had the same classes as the Wakka.

Each class-name had a feminine form in -gan in the tribes under notice.

To one or other of these four classes every individual belonged by birth, *the child's class being invariably determined by the mother's class.*

The classes regulated marriage in the following way :—

Taking the Kabi tribe for illustration, a man of the Barang class had to marry a woman of the Bŏnda class, if available, but, failing a Bŏndagan, he could marry a Dhĕrwaingan. Similarly, a man of the Balkuin class had to marry a Dhĕrwaingan, if available ; but provided he could not obtain a Dhĕrwaingan, it was permissible for him to marry a Bŏndagan.

[1] Curr, *The Austr. Race*, vol. iii. p. 223.
[2] Mathews, *R. G. S. of Austr. Q.*, p. 82 *seq.*

Substituting Banjur for Balkuin, the same rule applies to the Wakka people.

The system may be put in tabular form, thus :—

Balkuin marries Dhĕrwain-gan,	children are	Bŏnda, Bŏnda-gan.
Barang ,,	Bŏnda-gan,	,,	Dhĕrwain, Dhĕrwain-gan.
Dhĕrwain ,,	Balkuin-gan,	,,	Barang, Barang-gan.
Bŏnda ,,	Barang-gan,	,,	Balkuin, Balkuin-gan.

The classes are arranged in two pairs, those which form a pair being prohibited from intermarrying.

Going only by such a table as that above, it is possible to arrange the classes in wrong pairs. The table shows that a Balkuin's son is Bŏnda, and a Barang's son Dhĕrwain. With imperfect knowledge, one might conclude that descent is patrilineal, because, thinking of father and children, it runs Balkuin, Bŏnda, Balkuin, Bŏnda, *ad lib.*, and so on with the other classes that are correspondingly related. This was Dr Howitt's interpretation. But so to conclude is to misapprehend the system. The correct way, the aboriginal way, of apprehending the descent in these tribes is to have regard to the class of the mother. Reckoning through the mother, the descent runs Bŏnda,

Dhĕrwain, Bŏnda, Dhĕrwain, *ad lib.*, and
Barang, Balkuin, Barang, Balkuin, *ad lib.*
The classes, therefore, that were paired
together and forbidden to intermarry were
Barang and Balkuin, on the one hand, and
Bŏnda and Dhĕrwain on the other. Substituting Banjur for Balkuin, the same remark
applies to the Wakka and the other tribes
having the Wakka class-names.

The two large moieties are conveniently
called phratries. The classes are divided
between them thus,

Phratry I.		*Phratry II.*	
Dilbai	{ Dhĕrwain Bŏnda	Kŏpaitthin	{ Barang Balkuin

Dilbai is often spelt Dilbi and Dilebi,
methods which do not make the terminal
diphthong distinct. That descent is reckoned
through the mother is absolutely certain from
the following considerations : (1) the way the
classes are paired : Dhĕrwain is not paired
with Barang nor Bŏnda with Balkuin, as in Dr
Howitt's arrangement ; (2) the option to marry
a member of the class paired with the proper
marrying class, in case a regular partner is not

available ; (3) the fact that the child's class has no reference to the father's class, but only to the mother's ; (4) the division of nature into two sections corresponding to the phratries in my arrangement.

Barang class married with Bŏnda class ; if the female were Bŏndagan class the child was of the Dhĕrwain class ; if the female were Barang-gan, the child was of the Balkuin class. Similarly, Balkuin class intermarried with Dhĕrwain class with corresponding descent of names. If a partner of the regular class was not available, it was lawful and common to mate with a member of the right phratry but of the other class. I have given the most exact information obtained from different sources as to the proper classes to intermarry. The children always belonged to the mother's phratry, and not to her own class but to the class paired with hers to form the phratry. Thus, I knew two men, Murudhalin and Bual, both belonging to the Barang class, whose children were respectively Bŏnda and Dhĕrwain. Why? Because the wives were respectively Dhĕrwain and Bŏnda. If descent had been patrilineal the children of these two

KAGARIU, OR JOHNNIE CAMPBELL, OF KABI TRIBE,
MARY RIVER, QUEENSLAND, THE MOST NOTORIOUS
NATIVE BUSHRANGER.

(Ætat. 24.)

Photo kindly supplied by Queensland Penal Dept.

To face p. 137.

families would have belonged to the one class. My maternal uncle was called a Barang because the leading local natives were Barang. My mother was therefore accounted a Barang-gan and I was a Balkuin. I belonged to the class paired with my mother's in her phratry.

The following two facts supply incidental proofs of the accuracy of the above explanation of the system. Kagariu, a Dhĕrwain, was getting the worst of it in a tussle with his gin. He saw two blacks approaching, one Waruin, a Balkuin, older than himself; the other, Turandiu, a Bŏnda, younger than himself. He called out for help, "Wuthung, Wuthung!" ("Younger brother, younger brother!") to the younger and weaker man as belonging to his phratry, the other would be counted a tribal brother of his wife. Two youths, Turandiu and Kilkoi, the one a Bŏnda, the other a Dhĕrwain, attempted to force an elderly woman, who was a Barang, and therefore belonged to the other phratry from theirs.

All the members of the one class, of the same generation, were reckoned as brothers and sisters. Even members of the same phratry, though of different classes, called

H

themselves brothers. The class-name was the commonest mode of address. They seemed to take a pleasure in calling one another Barang or Banjur, Bŏnda or Dhĕrwain. To marry within the one class, or to marry into the other class of one's own phratry was alike unlawful. I knew of no such marriage. Still cohabitation between members of classes not allowed to marry was not regarded, apparently, so heinous an offence in these tribes as in other parts of Australia. The union was not allowed to continue, but no penalty was inflicted.

In *Eaglehawk and Crow*, I propounded the hypothesis, that the intermarrying classes originally represented two different races. There seems to be no reason to doubt that where the classes are now four or even eight, they are merely a multiplication and development of two primary classes or phratries. The two divisions prevailing over a large part of New South Wales and Victoria were known by the aboriginal names for eaglehawk and crow respectively. In some parts, where the sections received other names, as Kurōkaity (Kurokaitch), white cockatoo, and Kapaity, black cockatoo (or long-billed cockatoo and

A COMPARATIVELY STRAIGHT-HAIRED AND A CURLY-HAIRED MAN.
Natives of Yabber, Kabi Tribe, Mary River, Queensland.

To face p. 138.

banksian cockatoo, according to Dawson)[1] in the west of Victoria and the adjoining portion of South Australia, the names implied a contrast in colour. My recent discovery of the meaning of the phratry names prevailing over the greater part of Queensland (communicated to the *Journ. of the R. Anthrop. Inst.*), has largely extended the known area over which the names of the phratries signified light and dark colour contrasted. These newly explained phratry names are Wutaru from *watta*, crow, and Yungaru from *yunga*, white cockatoo, varied in the north-west to Pakuta from *paku*, also meaning white cockatoo. Mr N. W. Thomas has rightly laid stress on the colour contrast involved in the animal names for the phratries in places very widely apart.[2] I suggested that the Crow class stood for the autochthonous Tasmanians, akin to the Papuans and Melanesians, and the Eaglehawk class for a more advanced, more powerful, lighter-coloured, straighter-haired race, physically resembling the Dravidians of India and the Veddahs of Ceylon, which gradu-

[1] *Austr. Abor.*, p. 27.
[2] *Kin. and Mar. in Austr.*, p. 53 *seq.*

ally immigrated by way of Cape York peninsula in the north-east, overcame and absorbed or exterminated the inferior autochthones. I further suggested that the multiplication of classes from two to four, and four to eight was due to an amalgamation of tribes, each having two or four classes, as the case might be, instancing such an amalgamation of two tribes, each having four classes, which is proceeding at the present time in Central Australia. The method of multiplication from two to four classes, I am disposed, however, to leave an open question.

It may be reasonably objected to the hypothesis that the two phratries represent two races, that two exogamous sections occur among other savages, *e.g.*, the Melanesians, of which it cannot be predicated that they represent an amalgamation of distinct races. In answer it may be said that even the Melanesians are not an absolutely homogeneous race. They are mixed to some extent with Polynesians: the islands of Tanna and Aniwa are only 14 miles apart. The natives of the one are Melanesians and of the other Polynesians. They are distinguishable by features and complexion as well as by language. And further, the Australian instance may explain the Melanesian rather than the converse. In any case, both instances will be due to like causes, though not necessarily to identical causes.

Corroboration of my hypothesis of the origin of the phratries has been supplied by Mrs Langloh Parker. She states that the two primary classes in the Euahlayi tribe were regarded as distinguished by difference in the colour of the blood, the phratry names begin Gwaigullean (light-blooded), and Gwaimudthen (dark-blooded).[1] Dr Andrew Lang[2] and Mr N. W. Thomas[3] have both commented upon this confirmation of my hypothesis.

On the occasion of my visit to Barambah, in October 1906, a station on the border of the Kabi and Wakka territories, I accidentally and unexpectedly discovered that these two tribes recognised the same distinction of lighter and darker blood as characterising the classes. The information was tendered quite spontaneously, without my having put any leading question. There was even a gradation re-

[1] *The Euah. Tr.*, p. 11.   [2] *Ibid.*, Introd., p. xxii.
[3] *Kin. and Mar.*, p. 53 *et seq.*

cognised in the shade of the blood of the four classes.

On a visit to Lake Condah Aboriginal Station in August 1907, I was surprised to meet the Kabi woman Tanggauwanan (Mrs MacDuff), who had been brought to Melbourne about 1870, and had remained in Victoria ever since. She had not forgotten her native tongue and was delighted to converse with me in it. She must be over sixty years of age.

Tanggauwanan gave me the two phratry names without my having mentioned them to her, and she identified the classes in relation to the phratries as indicated above.

Tanggauwanan confirmed the statement of an informant at Barambah, that Dilbai was the light-blood section, and Kŏpaitthin, the dark blood. But it should be stated that at Barambah there was difference of opinion as to which was which.

The names of the phratries have also been given to me in the forms Dilbaiin and Kŏpaiin.

The identification of the classes with particular castes and with blood distinctions is, as I have already shown, an old explanation,

dating at least from 1847, being mentioned
then by Leichhardt and others. But the conclusions as to castes were more conjectural than
well-founded. The correspondence of the
phratries with blood distinctions, has not, by
recent writers other than myself, been recognised
in Queensland. But as it obtains among the
Euahlayi, 300 miles distant in New South
Wales, and has been remarked by Mrs D. M.
Bates, in the extreme south-west of Australia,
it is reasonable to infer that difference of colour
in blood or complexion, or in both, is a very
ancient and widely diffused aboriginal explanation of the primary classes, and implies, in the
aboriginal mind, a traditional recognition of
fundamental racial differences amalgamated in
the Australians.

The distinction as to colour of blood, has,
theoretically, among the Kabi and Wakka, a
relation to colour of skin, and is not confined to
the classes in human society, but extends to the
animals grouped with the respective classes.
The colour of the skin is supposed to correspond to the colour of the blood. Such is the
theory, although the application of it seems
inconsistent. It is important to note a fact I

144 Two Tribes of Queensland

have already called attention to, viz., that the two classes which are paired together, forming a phratry, have a common relationship to the same sets of natural objects. I cannot say for certain that the whole of Nature is subjected to a dichotomous division, as was the case at Mt. Gambier, in South Australia, and also among the Euahlayi in New South Wales, but an immense number of objects in heaven and earth are distributed between the phratries, and, probably, all Nature, if not now allocated, was at one time so divided.

To Balkuin and Barang belonged, amongst other objects, the north wind, the emu, the white cockatoo, the carpet-snake, kīlla (dark-coloured native bee), dinda (the magpie lark), coal, red clay or paint, the bunya tree, the Moreton Bay ash and grass. To Dhĕrwain and Bŏnda belonged the sun, moon, stars, clouds, night, wind, thunder, lightning, water, the whale, the eaglehawk, the curlew, the black cockatoo, the dog, the "old man" kangaroo, the brown snake, the dark iguana, the ground iguana, kawai (the light-coloured native bee), and the deaf adder. The principle of division is far from obvious.

The connection between the human being and the natural objects belonging to his or her phratry, was regarded to be very intimate. Thus if a Barang or Balkuin wanted information about a friend, and saw a magpie lark, he would ask the little bird a question, such as, " Is my brother coming ? " and it would by its note give him a suitable and intelligible reply.

So far as I am aware, the restrictions about food were not dependent upon the classes, but were determined by other principles, such as age, sex, and occasions of mourning. Groups of persons stood in a common relationship to some particular totem, as distinct from the general phratric connection, a relationship derived hereditarily. The Kabi word for the totemic animal was *murang*, meaning flesh or animal. With this word may be compared the Bugandaity *tuman*, similarly employed and also meaning flesh or meat. A man was not debarred from killing and eating his totem, but in practice he protected it and regarded it as belonging to his own people. A person's totem was never changed.

It may be helpful to illustrate the phratry

and class relations by concrete examples. I subjoin the relationships of Tanggauwanan and several members of her family, giving particulars as far as available.

D. will stand for Dilbai phratry, and K. for Kŏpaitthin.

FIRST GENERATION.

Tanggauwanan's maternal grandfather; Dauwabŏra community, K. phratry, Barang class, Nguruin (emu), totem.

T.'s maternal grandmother; Patyala community of Frazer Island, D. phratry, Dhĕrwain-gan class, Muroirai (whipsnake), totem.

SECOND GENERATION.

T.'s father, Wanggūmbalu; Gundabŏra community, K. phratry, Balkuin class, Koroi (opossum), totem.

T.'s mother, Bŏndŏbin, Dunwabŏra community, D. phratry, Bŏndagan class, Muroirai (whipsnake), totem.

THIRD GENERATION.

Tanggauwanan; Gundabŏra community, D. phratry, Dhĕrwain-gan class, Muroirai (opossum) totem.

Yanbirinya (T.'s Kabi betrothed); Gigarbŏra community, K. phratry, Barang class, Nguruin (emu), totem.

T.'s brothers and sisters; Gundabŏra community, D. phratry, Dhĕrwain class, Muroirai (whipsnake), totem.

FOURTH GENERATION.

T.'s son (born in Victoria), D. phratry, Bŏnda class, Muroirai (whipsnake), totem.

The rule of matrilineal descent is clear. Tanggauwanan is Dhĕrwaingan, her brothers Dhĕrwain, her mother was Bŏndagan, her mother's mother Dhĕrwaingan. These all belonged to the Dilbai phratry. The community or bŏra, to which one belonged, was that of the father. The totem seems to have been transmitted by inheritance through the mother.

The following table, giving the phratries, classes, and totems of three families, shows clearly (1) that the Dilbai phratry is constituted by the Dhĕrwain and Bŏnda classes and the Kŏpaitthin phratry by the Barang and Balkuin classes ; (2) that descent is matrilineal ; and (3) that either class of one phratry may marry with either class of the other.

The meaning of the phratric and class-names is a matter of some importance. I have spelt the phratry names phonetically as exactly as I could. They are usually spelt Dilebi, or Dilbi, and Kupathin. Both names may be corrupt. The diphthong *ai* in Dilbai suggests to me the elision of a consonant between

INDIVIDUAL.	NATIVE NAME.	SECTION.	CLASS.	MURANG.
Arthur	Bujīrgundau	Dilbai	Dhĕrwain	Emu or Bunya ?
Arthur's wife	?	Kŏpaitthin	?	?
Peggy, Arthur's mother	?	Dilbai	Bŏndagan	Iguana or Turkey.
Arthur's father	Munojan	Kŏpaitthin	Balkuin	Kangaroo.
Peggy's father	Kuneraman	Kŏpaitthin	Barang	Carpet-snake.
Peggy's mother	?	Dilbai	Dhĕrwaingan	?
Jenny Lind (half-caste)	Māl	Kŏpaitthin	Baranggan	Bunya Tree.
J. L.'s mother, Kitty	…	Kŏpaitthin	Banjurgan	Bunya Tree.
J. L.'s husband, Mickey	Bulīr	Dilbai	Dhĕrwain	Kangaroo or Iguana.
Mickey's father	Kanan	Kŏpaitthin	Barang	Turkey.
Mickey's mother, Kitty	…	Dilbai	Bŏndagan	Kangaroo.
J. L.'s son, Ben	Buwanor	Kŏpaitthin	Banjur	Bunya Tree.
J. L.'s daughter, Mary	Maranger	Kŏpaitthin	Banjurgan	Bunya Tree.
Charles Beattie	Jianī	Dilbai	Joroin	Iguana.
C. B.'s wife, Aggie	Mujinbī	Kŏpaitthin	Banjurgan	Sugar-bag (Gayer).

the vowels. Such elisions are common in Australian dialects. There may be a similar elision in Kŏpaitthin. This surmise, if well founded, would imply earlier forms, such as Dilbari or Dilbara, and Kŏparitthin. As *d* and *k* frequently interchange, Dilbai may just be a variant of Kilpara (eaglehawk) of the Darling blacks. I suspect that Kŏpaitthin is radically the same as Kapaity (Kapaitch) of Victoria and South Australia, where it means banksia cockatoo and black cockatoo. The radical meaning of Kŏpaitthin may have reference to darkness of colour, and the word may therefore be applied to dark birds, such as the crow or black cockatoo.

Mr N. W. Thomas raises the important question, whether the particular phratry names correspond to anything existing in the pre-phratriac age.[1]

His conclusion that the eaglehawk-crow stories were originally independent of the phratry names, and prior to them, and that they referred to racial conflict, seems to harmonise with all the known facts. As Mr Thomas observes,[2] so far as the evidence

[1] *Kin. and Mar.*, p. 54 *seq.*   [2] *Ibid.*, p. 55.

adduced by me in *Eaglehawk and Crow* goes, bird-myths do not appear to be told outside Victoria and the Darling area of New South Wales. But negative evidence is usually inconclusive. In the chapter on "Myths and Legends" in this book will be found two versions of the myth I have called "The Spiteful Crow." These furnish proof that the conflict bird-myths were current in Queensland as far north as lat. 25°. This means that they occurred some 250 miles further north than hitherto discovered. It is interesting that a third version of the same story, was current in Victoria on the Lower Murray. Mrs D. M. Bates' forthcoming book on the aborigines of West Australia will supply evidence of bird-myths, in which the eaglehawk and crow both figure, having been told in that State. Mr Thomas' inference, from previous evidence, that these myths would probably be known all over Australia, is greatly corroborated by these discoveries of Mrs Bates and myself.

As regards the Kabi and Wakka class-names, the result of my inquiries is that Barang and Dhĕrwain both mean emu, and that Bŏnda means kangaroo, one informant said a long-

tailed kangaroo known as *wallan*. About the
meaning of Balkuin there was difference of
opinion. One informant gave it as native bear,
but I doubt the accuracy of this, for such
reasons as the following : At the junction of
the Thomson and the Barcoo, *balcun* stands
for kangaroo. For the Kabi term Balkuin
the tribes to the north, west and south sub-
stitute Bandur or Banjur, which may be a
variant of Kamilroi *bundar*, kangaroo. At the
Hastings River, in New South Wales, *bulkoing*
means red wallaby, and *bundarra* black wallaby.
Bŏnda (English spelling Bunda), with the
significance of kangaroo, occurs in a number
of New South Wales' dialects, and it is very
interesting to find the words *dirrawan*, emu,
and *bundar* (elsewhere *bundah*), kangaroo,
occurring together in the Kamilroi dialect at
Barraba, New South Wales.[1] It is singular
that each phratry should have an emu class
and a kangaroo class, also that the class-names
should have become specialised for the classes,
and their original meaning obscured if not
forgotten, other names being substituted to
designate the animals. Difference in colour

[1] Curr's *Austr. Race*, vol. iii. p. 320.

would explain the use of two names of marsupials, but not of two names for emu. The peculiar nomenclature favours the presumption that at a remote period each phratry may have occupied its own territory, as was the case in those parts of Victoria, where the natives born in one community were all Bunjil (eaglehawk), and in the other all Wa (crow) ; the communities being exogamous, the wives were always of the phratry different to that of both their husbands and children. Of course, with the Kabi and Wakka, the husband and father is of the one phratry, while the wife and children belong to the other.

CHAPTER IX

THE FAMILY, KINSHIP AND MARRIAGE

THE family, consisting of husband and wife, or wives, with their children, constituted a distinct social unit. They occupied the same gunyah (dwelling), they ate together, they travelled together. The wife was the regular nurse of the infants, but the husband occasionally took a turn. In the family, where there were children, three classes would be represented, the father's, the mother's and the children's, the children always belonging to the class that was of the same phratry with the class of their mother.

Children were over-indulged. Husbands were usually affectionate to their wives, but when angered they were often brutal, thrashing them unmercifully with waddies, sometimes breaking their limbs and cracking their skulls. Still the conjugal bond generally held out for a lifetime.

The classes were exogamous but not necessarily the tribes.

The following table, arranged in squares, in

four generations, shows certain family relationships, with their Kabi names.

KABI TERMS OF KINSHIP—*Two Phratries with Two Classes each.*

GENER.	CLASS B₁.	PHRATRY B (CLASS B)	CLASS A₁.	PHRATRY A (CLASS A)
I.	*Yēman* (mother's mother) *Maiŏin* (father's father and father's brother)		*Ngathang* (mother's father) *Kŏmarŏm* (father's mother)	
II.		*Ngavang* (mother) „ *Kŏmī* (mother's sister) (mother's brother) „ (wife's father)		*Pabun* (father) „ (father's brother) *Yuruin* (wife's mother) *Nyulang* (father's sister)
III.	EGO. *Nun* (elder brother) *Wuthung* (younger brother) *Yabun* (elder sister) *Naibar* (younger sister)		*Malingan* (wife) *Yūmo* (father's sister's son) *Yūmon* (father's sister's daughter)	
IV.		*Kani* (sister's son) *Kaningan* (sister's daughter)		*Kani* (son) *Kaningan* (daughter)

TERMS OF KINSHIP

Kabi Terms

My father.   Pabun.

„ father's brother.   Pabun.

„ mother's sister's husband.   Pabun.

„ mother.   Ngavang or Ngabang.

„ mother's sister.   Ngavang or Ngabang.

„ father's second wife.   Ngavang or Ngabang.

„ stepmother.

„ father's sister.   Yuruin.

„ mother's brother's wife.   Yuruin.

„ mother's brother.   Kŏmī.

„ father's sister's husband.   Kŏmī.

„ son or daughter.   s. Kanī, d. Kanīngan.

„ brother's child (I being male) { s. Kanī, d. Kanīngan, also Kumma.

„ brother's child (I being female).   Kanī, Kanīngan.

„ sister's child (I being male).   Kanī, Kanīngan.

„ sister's child (I being female).   Kanī, Kanīngan.

„ elder brother.   Nun.

„ elder sister.   Yabun.

„ younger brother.   Wuthung.

„ younger sister.   Naibar.

„ father's brother's child.   Yumō, m. Yumŏn, f.

„ mother's sister's child { older Nun, m.   Yabun, f. younger   Wuthung,   m. Naibar, f.

„ father's father.   Maibīn.

„ father's father's brother.   Maibīn.

„ father's father's sister.   Nundai (?) also Maibīn.

„ father's mother.   Kŏmarŏm also Maiyirŏm (?)

„ father's mother's brother.   Nyundai.

My father's mother's sister. Kŏmarŏm.

„ mother's mother. Yĕnan or Yĕnanbarŏm.

„ mother's mother's brother. Kŏmarŏm.

„ mother's mother's sister. Yĕnan.

„ mother's father. Ngathang or Ngathŏmbarŏm.

„ mother's father's brother. Ngathang or Ngathŏm-barŏm.

„ mother's father's sister. Ngathang or Ngathŏm-barŏm.

„ father's sister's child. Yumō, m. Yumŏn, f.

„ mother's brother's child. Yumō, m. Yumŏn, f.

A widower. Burong or Burŏndŏm.

„ widow. Kulun.

A father-in-law. Kŏmī.

„ mother-in-law. Nyulanggan.

„ son-in-law. Nyulang.

„ daughter-in-law. Kŏlanmīn.

„ husband. Malithanmī or Dhandōr.

„ wife. Malimgan or Malimin-gan.

The above terms appear to have originated from the union in marriage of two families of brothers and sisters, and indicate that the usual matches were between cousins. In the terms designating the more distant relatives there may be some error, but the terms for the nearer relatives are almost certainly all correct. I am not aware of any error, but I had three lists and where there were discrepancies I have given the terms from the most reliable list.

The eligibles for marriage may be thus shown :—

Ego (male) Balkuin	My mother Baranggan	my Ngabang
	Her brother Barang	my Kŏmī
	His wife Bŏndagan	my Yuruin
	Their daughter Dhĕr-wain-gan	my Yumŏn (eligible) Wife
Ego (female) Balkuin-gan	Their son Dhĕrwain	my Yumō (eligible) Husband
Mother, etc., as above.		

The following unions are also permissible :—

Ego (male) Balkuin	My father Dhĕrwain	my Pabun
	His sister Dhĕrwain-gan	my Yuruin
	Her husband Balkuin	my Kŏmī
	Their daughter Bŏndagan	my Yumŏn(permissible) Wife
Ego (female) Balkuin-gan	Their son Bŏnda	my Yumō (permissible) Husband,
Father, etc., as above.		

The terms of relationship necessarily fit into the classes but, according to my view, they preceded the class distinctions, and some of them were later extended by analogy to all the members of a class.

The theory of group marriage has received very influential support among Australian anthropologists. Drs. Fison and Howitt first adopted it under the name of communal marriage, and Professor Spencer has endorsed it. According to this theory, originally there was unregulated promiscuity of intercourse, and, observing the evils resultant, the community took counsel together and divided itself into two sections, enacting a law of perpetual obligation, that sexual intercourse should not take place within the section, but that the members of the one section or group should have common conjugal rights over the other. Dr Howitt's hypothesis, that the idea of making such a division might have come to some wizard as a fancied revelation from a supernatural being in the dreams of the night, and then might have been enforced by the collusion of other wizards with him,[1] seems to me very fanciful and far-fetched. It would involve the conclusion that a similar dream came to similar wizards among the Melanesians, the Todas, etc., who also have two exogamous sections.

As communal marriage, on the large hypothetical scale, has never been known to exist, the term group marriage has been substituted,

[1] *Nat. Tr. of S.-E. Austr.*, pp. 89, 90, 143.

being supposed to receive support from existing practices and names of kin relationships in certain tribes. This theory of group marriage by enactment reminds one of the old theory of the origin of language by convention. However it came about that there now exist classes, the members of which are eligible to intermarry, *i.e.*, the members of the one to marry the members of the other, and classes the members of which are conceived as standing in fraternal relation to each other and are ineligible to intermarry, I ask, is it not more in harmony with the recognised development of human society, and therefore more scientific, to assume that such a class relationship grew unconsciously, gradually, and naturally out of the actual relations of small family groups, or was the outcome of the contact of distinct races, or originated partly by the one cause, partly by the other, than to propound a theory, which requires savage man to discover hypothetical evil results from incest (supposed evils which have no real existence), and to enact a statute as a remedy, which he had neither the capacity to invent nor the power to carry into effect if invented ?

As we have seen, the Kabi and Wakka tribes regarded the members of a class as of the same blood colour, and, inferentially, of the same skin colour. Light blood married dark blood. According to one statement the lighter class of the light-blood phratry married the lighter class of the dark-blood phratry, and the darker class of the light-blood phratry married the darker class of the dark-blood phratry. But within these broad distinctions there were other considerations which regulated marriage. The Kabi people have two verbs which denote marrying, *bindamathī*, to marry, with proper consent of guardians, and *dhŏmmamathī*, to marry without consent, or by capture. When the first mode was followed, the girl was given away by her brother or other male guardian, from goodwill, or in exchange for another bride, and the whole transaction was amicably conducted. When the second form was adopted, the man who annexed the woman had to atone for his fault or temerity, and run the risk of losing her, by engaging in combat. Thus, the first husband of Jenny Lind, a half-caste already mentioned, was an aboriginal named Mickey, who had to fight either her guardian or her betrothed, I forget which, for having taken possession of her without due consent.

Some have contended that the prevalence of marriage by capture among the Australians has been exaggerated. I doubt this. There are strong arguments in favour of the once extensive prevalence of this form of marriage. Let me mention one. The Rev. N. Hey, of Mapoon, Batavia River, Queensland, gives as the equivalent for husband in the Nggerikudi language, *danu-prange* (my man who caught me).[1]

If the two primary classes represent two primeval races, we can easily understand how marriage by capture might be a very common form of connubium.

There were occasions when some right, analogous to the *jus primæ noctis*, seems to have been exacted among the Kabi, by the seniors in the camp, but they point as much to former claims resulting from a joint-capture as to a former community of conjugal rights. The opinion of William Hopkins, a man who had an aboriginal partner, was that none but the husband had any matrimonial rights over the wife, and that jealousy made him take good

[1] *N. Queensland Ethn. Bull*, No. 6, p. 6.

care she was not interfered with, unless he were a consenting party. Sometimes, he said, a strange gin would be captured and taken to the camp by a blackboy, who having no great regard for her would throw her over as common property. She generally escaped to her own kindred at the first opportunity.

The elder men had sometimes a plurality of wives, while the young men had for a long time after reaching manhood to remain, perforce, single. I never knew a man to have more than two wives at the one time, and generally one sufficed. There was no minimum age for the marriage of girls, and so it occasionally happened that a child of twelve became the wife of a man of sixty. I knew a case in point.

The word in Kabi for wife is *malimgan.* Equivalents for husband are *malithanmī* (variant *malithinmin*), and *dhandōr.* There is a word *Kubikanman*, which seemed to me to express the idea of paramour. I merely mention it as a starting-point for further enquiry.

In Wakka, *nyōm* signifies husband, and *nyōmgan* wife. As -gan is the feminine suffix, *nyōm*, like English "spouse," must have a meaning applicable to both sexes.   The same remark applies to *malī, or malim*, in the Kabi words for husband and wife.

On the death of her husband, a widow belonged to his brother, or nearest male relative, who might retain her or give her away to a friend of the proper class.

The relationship of mother-in-law and son-in-law entailed the same kind of mutual avoidance as in other Australian tribes.   Custom forbade these relatives to look at one other.   If a man saw his wife's mother approaching, he turned his back upon her to avoid seeing her, or one or other of them would cover the head with a 'possum rug.   The relationship was indicated by the word *nyulang*.   The man was *nyulang*, the woman *nyulanggan*.   A variant of the same word described the same relationship in Victoria, over a thousand miles distant, as well as in other places.   Mr Parker says of the Jajowerong tribe in Victoria : " A stupid custom existed among them, which they called ' Knaloyne.'   Whenever a female child was promised in marriage to any man, from that very hour neither he nor the child's mother were permitted to look upon or hear each other speak nor hear their names mentioned by others ; for, if they did, they would immediately grow prematurely old and die." [1]

If we could explain the meaning of *nyulang* we might get some light on the origin of those "strained relations." The Rev. Dr Macdonald gives the radical meaning of a corresponding word in Efatese as "bowing" or "crouching." [2] This meaning implies the fact of concealment, but does not suggest the motive for it. Elsewhere I have suggested that probably in cases of marriage by capture it might have fallen to the girl's mother, as her natural guardian, to inflict some condign penalty upon the abductor, if he should happen to be overtaken, and that in the course of time the exaction of penalty was dispensed with and the fiction of mutual invisibility was introduced instead. [3] Since I made this suggestion I have learned that at Esperance Bay, if a young man absconded with a bespoken girl, both offenders were killed if captured. [4]

[1] R. B. Smyth's *Abor. of Vic.* vol. ii. p. 156.
[2] *Oc. Langs.*, p. 206. [3] *Eag. and Cr.*, p. 115.
[4] *Tr. R. Soc. S. Austr.*, vol. xvi. p. 281.

This avoidance, suggesting an old-time hostility, is in accord with certain practices accompanying wedlock in civilised society, such as throwing shoes at a departing bridal pair, for which our further refinement has substituted confetti. These customs, inexplicable on the surface, are now recognised as surviving evidences of a previous condition of conflict and enmity. Prof. A. H. Keane mentions an analogous practice that persisted until recently in Patagonia. "On the death of any young person the head of the family was required to despatch some aged woman, a mother-in-law by preference. Hence, through fear of such a fate, women acquired the habit of avoiding all contact with their sons-in-law, and the feeling continued after the motive had been forgotten." [1]

The number of children in a family was small on the average. Six would be rare. I knew of no aboriginal family with more than five who survived infancy. The half-caste Jenny Lind had nine, but her fertility was probably inherited from the European side. Infanticide must have been freely practised.

[1] *Ethn.*, p. 219.

A gin called Dwangin was said to have murdered all her offspring.

The motive for infanticide with these tribes could not be to save food in times of dearth, for the food supply was constant and plentiful. It would be mainly, if not entirely, that mothers might escape the irksomeness of nursing and caring for infants and of carrying them on their frequent journeys.

A new-born child, instead of being washed, was fortified against the risks to life by being smeared all over with a mixture of powdered charcoal and fat.

CHAPTER X

RELIGION AND MAGIC

THE relation of religion to magic has, in recent years, assumed an immense importance, thanks largely to the writings of Dr J. G. Frazer and Dr Andrew Lang. Dr Frazer holds that religion is the outcome of despair in the efficacy of magic, and as the Australians are all firm believers in magic and habitually practise it, he necessarily asserts that they have not yet arrived at the stage which discards magic for religion.

Had the Kabi and Wakka tribes any religion? Our answer depends upon our definition of religion. If we accept Dr Frazer's definition, which makes the offering of propitiatory rites to supernatural beings an essential element, the conclusion, perhaps, must be that these tribes were destitute of religion. I say perhaps, because although I never heard from the natives of rites which could be called propitiatory, yet there may have been rare and informal examples of such rites. For instance, in Victoria, a sorcerer was in the habit of cutting off some of his own hair, and this, greased with some kidney fat of a human victim, whom he had murdered some time previously, he would cast into the River Murray to purchase the favour of a water spirit.[1] And Mrs D. M. Bates has shown that the blacks in the south-west of West Australia throw rushes and branches upon certain sacred spots to mollify the spirits that haunt them. Such acts may be accurately described as conciliatory rites. And it may be laid down as axiomatic that in Australia no definite aboriginal custom is confined to one locality. It will crop up, perhaps slightly varied, five hundred or a thousand miles away. I am not aware, however, of the practice of such conciliatory acts among the tribes now under notice, if we exclude the alleged transactions with Dhakkan, the rainbow, to be described later. And yet I would say that these tribes possessed the elementary contents of religion. They acknowledged the existence of supernatural beings, who had power to render assistance or inflict

[1] Beveridge, *Abor. of Vic.*, p. 97.

injury. They spoke of them with reverence. They also believed in the continued existence of the *nguthuru*, or "shades" of human beings after death. These *nguthuru* could occasionally be seen, with smiling countenances, as they floated among the foliage at night and peered down upon their quondam fellow-mortals.

The references to some of the supernatural beings are, unfortunately, very vague and fragmentary. It is probably too late to gather distinct impressions and thoroughly accurate knowledge on beliefs about such beings after the natives have had nigh sixty years of intercourse with the whites with concurrent decadence of virility and gradual desuetude of customs.

One of their conceptions was that of a great supernatural being who was nameless. He was referred to only, with bated breath, as *Ngunda, i.e.*, he, like the "that," the supreme âtman of the Brahmans. This spirit was vast and wonderful. An old gin expressed the relation of her people to him this way: "*Ngundanō branga*" ("[People] must be thinking of Ngunda [Him]").

K

Ngunda, although remarkable, was not the greatest of spirits. *Bīral*, in Wakka *Bīra*, was morally better, and in size more huge. In fact, he was the greatest spirit. Tanggauwanan told me she got to know about *Bīral* in this way. She was once playing about a huge flat rock and she asked her mother, "Who put the stone here?" Her mother replied, "*Bīral*." "Who is *Bīral*?" she asked. "He lives up there," said her mother. "What is it? Is it like you and me?" "Wa ngatyu nŏmngathi, bŏna ngalīn nyāgō." ("I have not seen [him]; by-and-by we shall see [him]"), was the reply.

I was told that the first people had seen *Bīral*.

Another variety of supernatural being had representatives of both sexes. Jŏnjarī (male), and Jŏnjarĭngan (female), who were acknowledged by both tribes. They were benevolent spirits, whose haunts were mineral springs. The healthful influences of the springs were ascribed to them. They protected the blacks, and rendered them happy. After initiation to manhood at the Kīvar-yĕngga (Man-making) the young man became jŏnjarīman, that is, he

enjoyed the favour of the Jŏnjarī. This fact
suggests that in the initiation ceremonies, if
the Jŏnjarī were not expressly invoked, some
reference was made to them. These spirits
bestowed upon the natives magic stones known
as *kundīr* in Kabi, *nurum* in Wakka, and also
cord or rope called *bukkur* (*bukkurumbil*, in
Wakka), both of which objects had the power
of conferring extraordinary vitality. The
kundīr were, no doubt, quartz crystals.

Dhakkan, or Takkan, was the most distinctly
imaged supernatural being. This was the
name for the rainbow, with which the spirit was
identified. In form he was a combination of
fish and snake. His abodes were the deepest
waterholes. When visible as a rainbow, he
was supposed to be passing from one waterhole
to another. He possessed terrific power, so
that he could shatter the scrubs and mountains.
He could also slaughter human beings if so
disposed. At times he was tricky and
malignant. It was he who substituted *tsīkoi*
(half-castes) for pure-bred, aboriginal infants.
The blacks therefore called him *warang*, *i.e.*,
wicked. But he could do a good turn to men
already possessed of some magical faculty.

The man who was *kundīr - bŏnggan*, many-crystalled, *i.e.*, who had many crystals within his body, would lie down to sleep on the margin of Dhakkan's watery dwelling. He would become dimly conscious of a prickly sensation in his limbs. We have felt it ourselves, when camping out and our circulation has become sluggish through cold. Then Dhakkan had taken him down into his domain and had effected a grand exchange. The blackfellow imparts *kundīr* to Dhakkan and the latter confers *bukkur* in return. The man is then laid to rest again upon the edge of the waterhole, and when he wakes up, he is *manngurngur*, *i.e.* full of life. Through this transaction with Dhakkan he is now a sorcerer of the highest degree. This exchange is analogous to a belief which Spencer and Gillen refer to. They, however, understand that the aborigine is supposed to disembowel himself entirely or partially, whereas in the Kabi-Wakka conception, he only parts with *kundīr*. The Dhakkan spirit, or being, was also recognised by the Turubul tribe of the Brisbane River, whose territory lay immediately south of the Kabi country. Dhakkan was regarded as the repository of crystals as well as rope, and would also dispense them on occasions.

One variety of spirits was purely malignant. These were the *Ubi* (*Malung* in Wakka), who creep about and prompt people to do wrong. At the head of the Mary River there is a station called Oobi Oobi, the name being associated with a haunt of these spirits.

Nguthuru in Kabi, *Ngul* in Wakka, was the regular word for the shadow of any object. It came to be specialised as the name for a ghost or phantom. There was no well-defined idea about future existence, but there was a belief that the dead became *Nguthuru*, or that the *Nguthuru* of the living survived death, and frequented the treetops. They were regarded as being sufficiently substantial to be able to answer a cooey addressed to them.

The belief in the efficacy of magic is universal among the Australians: even Christianised blacks cannot shake it off. One such, in Victoria, told me about a native wizard who could produce abundance of fine water where none was either visible or supposed to exist. Every native was considered capable of practising magic, and no doubt all would try it

at some time or other. It was usually practised
with malicious intent, and the dread of it must
have frequently caused sickness and death.
But by the recognised sorcerers magic was
utilised as a healing art as well as for destructive
ends.

We have seen that the influence or inspira-
tion of the Jŏnjarī conferred magical faculty,
but the secret of the sorcerer's power was
generally regarded as the possessing, within
his body, magical stones, which were of two
kinds. The one sort known as nganpai, or
kundīr, already referred to, was a large, white,
quartz crystal. The other sort, called minkŏm,
was described as being flat, circular and of a
black colour. I have seen specimens of the
latter kind in Victoria, like a convex lens,
about 1 inch in breadth and ¾ inch thick in the
middle. A few have been found much larger.
They are marked with sinuous striations and
have the lustre of glittering black coal. Some
are oblong with rounded ends and about 1½
inch. long and ½ inch thick. The minkŏm
appear to have been those objects of obscure
origin known as obsidianites.

The sorcerer was believed to have a supply

of dhakkē (stones) within him,—the more he
had so much the greater his vitality and magic
power. He also had a stock, tangible and
visible, for use with his hands. These he
carried in his nguam manggurngur (vital bag),
vulgarly known as a saucy dillie-bag. This
receptacle of the artillery of sorcery was about
the size and shape of an opera-glass case, and
had a cord attached, by which it was carried
slung over the shoulder. Although supposed
to be of supernatural origin, and to have been
fished out of water, it had all the appearance of
a hand-made article, just like other bags close-
netted with cord. However, there was no
limit to the credulity that attached to the
nguam, or ngunggaran, and its contents. In
addition to the stones, which were wrapped
round with hair or with string made of
squirrel's fur, a nguam would contain bones
and other relics of the dead, and, possibly,
hair, or excrement of some individual against
whom bodily mischief was determined.
Once, when visiting a camp, I saw a nguam
hanging from a tree. When I approached
to inspect it, the blacks, solicitous for my
safety, uttered a warning cry. No native

would dare to approach, touch or inspect a wizard's nguam.

To attain the highest degree of proficiency in sorcery, one required to have received from Dhakkan, the rainbow, either kundīr (crystals) or yurū (rope), the latter known also as bukkūr. How Dhakkan imparts yurū has already been described. Before the traffic with Dhakkan, the native may be only a Kundīr Bŏng-gan, but after it he is a full-blown Manngur. He is also said to be murū murū (*full of life*). Forthwith he is invulnerable and has enormous powers. One man I knew had given evidence of his being a Kundīr Bŏng-gan by his being bullet-proof on the occasion of an attack made on the camp by the native police. Once, when a boy was angry at me, he said, " Me tell im my daddy make im thunder and lightning come up alonga you." The same boy told me that one time when the black police suddenly raided the camp, a Manngur caught him up and tossed him through the air a mile or two into the scrub, then vanished underground and made his way to the same place of safety. He could have flown through space with equal ease.

The sorcerers were the chief physicians. The

crystals were called into requisition for remedial purposes.

The doctor would also apply one of the magic stones to a spot that was aching and afford the patient immediate relief by extracting from him a piece of glass or newspaper, a few yards of hair-string or even a quid of tobacco. A man with such powers was obviously a person of great consequence, to be propitiated and dreaded.

Some virtue appears to have resided in stones other than those used regularly in magic. I remember seeing a large piece of white quartz, that had become fixed in the fork of a tree by the tree's natural growth. Kilkoi, the boy who had originally placed it in this position, told me not to touch it, because doing so would cause rain.

When a person is killed, or supposed to be killed, by an unknown enemy, sometimes the body is roasted, a strip of skin is cut from the thigh and rolled round a spear, then, presumably by pointing the spear in all directions, it indicates who has caused the fatality.

The aversion of the blacks to pass under a rail or a leaning tree is well known. When I

inquired the reason, I was told it was owing
to the fear that the blood of a woman might
have been upon the wood, and that some
might fall upon the person passing underneath.
Men had a peculiar dread of contact with the
blood of a woman. For this reason the ornamental scars on women were cut by their own
sex. And on occasions such as childbirth,
when there was hæmorrhage, the woman was
secluded and not allowed to handle food for
the use of others. A man would not touch
anything she had touched. Before admission
to the camp, she had to destroy articles that
had come in contact with her and cover herself
with earth. When in the camp, a woman must
beware of touching a man with her feet and of
allowing her shadow to fall upon him. Failure
in these respects would bring sickness upon
him. Once when I inadvertently stepped over
a man, who was lying down, he flared up and
maledicted me for a stupid white fellow. Such
facts suggest the inference that the nguthuru
(shadow) had some potency for evil.

CHAPTER XI

THAT the Australian natives possessed a vast store of myths and legends is evident from the large number that have been already rescued from oblivion. Many of them were handed down in a rhythmical form, whole or in part, and were therefore easily committed to memory and easily recalled.

Stories like those which follow give a very accurate reflection of aboriginal life. They often show great tenderness, and are lightened by humorous touches. They contain ancient biographical notices and fading memories of tribal history, and in many cases they are the attempts of the native philosopher or naturalist to account for origins.

Some of the legends, or portions of them, I took down in the native dialects, believing that in this form they would be of value to the philologist. The very vocables, in places, have a delightful quaintness. As far as I have been able, I have given an accurate translation. For the titles I am responsible.

It will be observed that the same story assumes different features in different dialects. I would specially direct attention to the two versions of the tale that I have named " The Spiteful Crow." This is one of the " conflict " myths. Each version contributes special points of interest and helps both to round off and to interpret the tale.

How the Yuangan (Dugong) and the Kakar (Porcupine) changed Skins

A long time ago Yuangan and Kakar were comrades, and one day Yuangan said :

	" Ngara !	yō,	kŏla	yan-gō	kui ! "
	" Hi !	I say,	yonder	I'm going	hi ! "
Kakar.	" Wendyō	ngalīn		yan-gō ? "	
	" Where	(shall) we		go ? "	
Y.	" Kŏla	ngalīn	yĕna,		
	" Yonder	(let) us	go,		
	kungorgō	katyīnda	yīnman."		
	to the water	and there	go in."		
K.	" Kalangur ! "				
	" Good ! "				

_Y._   " Karī   yīnman   ngalīn   kai."
           " This way   go   we   here."

_K._   " É,   é ! "
           " Very well,   very well ! "

so off they set together.

When they got up next morning Yuangan asked again :

           " Ngara !   wendyō   ngalīn   yan-gō ? "
           " Hi !   where   (shall) we   go ? "

_K._   " Wenyiragō   ngalīn ? "
       " Where indeed   (shall) we ? "

_Y._   " Kībinya   warabam."
       " We are   getting tired."

_K._   " Wanyiram   ngindu   brangam ? "
       " Which way   (do) you   think ? "

_Y._   " Ngalīn   wendya   yan-gō ? "
       " We   wherever (shall)   go ? "

_K._   " Ngara !   ngalīn   wutyangalī."
       " Hi !   (let) us   make an attempt."

_Y._   " Ngai   .   tumu   wŏndam,
       " (Well) I (will)   tree   climb,
        ngai   tumu   nyinam.
        I (will)   in a tree   live."

_K._   " Ngathī."
       " Go on."

_Y._   " Ngai   wutyanongalīn."
       " I (will)   try."

K. "Ya, wŏnda ngin."
"Yes, climb you."

Yuangan then tried to climb the tree but alas

"bugī buming."
"(he) came tumbling down."

K. "Wenyari?"
"How are you getting on?"

Y. "Bumī ngai, bumī ngai."
"Fallen I, fallen I."

K. "Ngai yīkī."
"I (will try the) same."

Y. "É, é, ngin yīkī."
"Good, good, you too (try)."

Kakar attempted to climb but down he fell likewise and cried out—

"Warang ngai bumī."
"Badly (have) I fallen."

Y. "Ngara!"
"Hi!"

K. "A!"
"Well!"

Y. "Ngai kungī yanman wutyangalin."
"I in the water will go (and) try (there)."

K. "Athī!"
"Good!"

Y. "Ngin karinda nyinna."
"You here stop."

As Yuangan was *going into the water, he*
said :

    "Talī   ngai   kŏrī   korimgai
    "Now   I (am)   here   diving (through to the other
                                                waterhole),

        kŏla   ngai   wurubŏkan   kunga karvana."
        there   I (shall)   come out of the water other."

K.   " Athī,   wutyangaalī."
        "Well   (go on)   try."

Y.   "Nakan   ngindu   ngŏna."
        "Look   you (at)   me."

Then Yuangan plunged in and disappeared.
After a moment up he came at the other waterhole, panting and calling out :

    "Ngara !   kai   ngai."
    "Haloo !   here   I (am)."

K.   "O !   arīrŏm   kalangur   ngin   ngindī.
        "Oh !   wonderful,   capital   you   really.

             Yabuai   bŏka."
             Come   back again."

Y.   "Yakan   nya   ngindu,   nŏkka ! "
        " Here I go   look   you,   see ! "

K.   "Athī."
        "All right (go on)."

Then Kakar says to himself, as he looks
down :

    "Winya   ngunda   wabŏkam   ngindī ?
    "Wherever   (is) he   coming out   really ?

    "Kamiyan   ngundakan   ngindī."
    "Head first   he is coming   oh, oh ! "

Out came Yuangan panting, and as he lay down on the bank, he asked :

"Ngara! wenyari ngai?"
"I say! how (did) I (do it)?"

K. "Kalangur ngin arīrŏm. Ngin
 "Splendid you (are) wonderful. (Now) you

   yĕna karī, kila ngin yĕna,
   go in here, right away there you go,

   gurubŏkan tingīra kungga ya
   come out (at the) sea water yes

   ngin bukai bŏka."
   you back come."

So off went Yuangan under land and water to the sea and soon returned.

Y. "Ngara! kai ngai."
 "Hi! here I (am)."

K. "Ngara! wanyiragō?"
 "Hi! where shall I go?"

Y. "Wenya ngin yan-gō arīrŏm?"
 "Where (shall you) go dear me?"

K. "Ngara! ngai kalī wŏndam
 "I say! I (shall) yonder climb

   tunba."
   (the) mountain."

Away went Kakar to the mountain and there he found a hollow log and he said to himself:

"Karī ngai wutyanangalīgō."
"Here I shall have a try."

When he had got into the log he said :

> " Wanyiragō   ngai   ngindē   buka-kurīgō ?
> " How ever   (shall) I   really   turn-round ?
>
> Ngai   kalangur   kurīgō,   kalangur
> I (can)   first-rate   turn,   first-rate
> ngindī."
> really."

When he came out of the log he went to where he had left Yuangan, and shouted—

> " Wenya ? "
> " Where ? "

Y.   " O ! "
    " Here (I am)."

K.   " É,   é ! "
    " Very well, very well."

Y.   " Wendya yanmathī ? "
    " Where did you go ? "

K.   " Kalangur   atyu   batyimī,   arīrŏm."
    " First-rate   I   got on,   dear, dear."

Y.   " Minyanu   nyĕnam ? "
    " What place   are you going to stay at ? "

K.   " Nŏllanō   karimī   tumō."
    " Into a hole   I enter   in a log."

Y.   " Nganna   ngindu   kubar   yarī   wa."
    " Me   you   (your) skin   here   give."

K.   " É,   é."
    " Very good, very good."

Y.   " Kanga   ngindu."
    " Take   you (mine)."

L

So he strips off his skin and hands it to Kakar, who says—

"Kai   nginyŏnggai,"
"Here   (is yours),"

as he hands Yuangan his skin, adding,

"Ngin kungga   yĕna   ngai   kai   yĕnin,
"You to the water   go   I   here   (shall) go,

              kalangur tunbanī   yanman."
      it's fine on the mountain   strolling."

Y.   "Athī,   wŏnai   atyu   nginna."
       "Well,   leave   I   you."

K.   "Athī,   ngai   yīkī,   kai   yanin."
       "Well,   I   also,   good-   bye (lit. here I go)."

That was how Yuangan and Kakar exchanged their skins.

THE ORIGIN OF FIRE.

At one time Mundulum (the deaf adder), had the sole possession of fire, which he kept securely in his inside. All the birds tried in vain to get some of it, until the small hawk came along and played such ridiculous antics that Mundulum lost his gravity and began to laugh. Then the fire escaped from him and became common property.

THE FASTIDIOUS GRANDSON, OR WOULDN'T-EAT LOST HIS MEAT.

A Wakka Story.

Gutya, the sugar-bag, or native bee, had its nest in a wumgī tree, which grows in the scrub. A small brown hawk called Kakara was walking along one day and met his weandam (grandmother). The weandam sent him further on and he began to cry out—

"Wumgī, wumgī,   mutya ngarī   kutya bān-gē."
"Wumgī, wumgī,   there our   honey stands."

Then he saw some water and went back and called his grandmother—

"Weandam!"

She replied—

"O!"
"Well!"

Then he said—

"Gunggan   karangam   yunan."
"Here's water   here   (We'll) camp."

So there they made their camp for the night. Next morning the grandson was taking the dog with him to go out hunting, "Weandam," he said—

"Atyu   bugīnyabilē   bīnurū."
"I   shall take the dog   to get a bandicoot."

Then he called the dog—

> "Ai   Irībiraigō ! "
> "Come here   Irībiraigō ! "

When they got away from the camp, the boy told the dog to look out for bīnur (bandicoots). The dog ran scenting about and found something and barked for the boy to come. When Kakara came, what did he see but a kulim (a little brown lizard). He thought the dog had made a fool of him, so he cried out to it—

> "Nyulabai   ngin."
> "Told a lie you."

He brought the kulim home to his weandam and said—

> " Bugīnyi   yai."
> " The dog   has told a lie."

She said—

> " Atyu   ngwau,"
> " I   will cook it,"

and the grandmother cooked the lizard. The little boy couldn't stomach it, so she ate it all herself and thus Wouldn't-eat lost his meat.

THE COMBAT BETWEEN THE CROW AND THE EAGLEHAWK.

The Crow challenged the Eaglehawk to fight, and kept calling out—

"Yuang, yuanggō bauwarī mŏramai."
"Come up, come up, on the fighting-ground yonder."

"Yagobī, yagobī."
"Come along, come along."

And the Eaglehawk was answering—

"Kŏnna būnma, burajī, burajī, tautau, bīru, bīru."
"With the spear I will strike."

Then they went at it pell-mell and the Crow killed the Eaglehawk.

THE RIVALS.

The Bŏnyī (bunya) and the Kuloloi (cypress pine) being rivals, at one time had a great fight. Said Kuloloi:

"Wenyō ngālibō bun-gō nyanandigō?"
"Where (are) we the fight going to have?"

Bŏnyī—

"Kŏrange nyanandī Korawīga."
"There is the place at Frazer Island."

Then they began to fight and Bŏnyī speared

Kuloloi low down, hence all its lower branches
are like spears. As for Bŏnyī, it was speared
high up, which accounts for the lower part of
the stem being clear of branches to this day.

THE REVENGEFUL LOVER, OR HOW THE NICKS CAME ON THE WILD PLUM.

There was once a Bŏnyī that fell in love
with a dainty little tree called Kulvain, which
bore a bluish-black fruit like a plum. So he
went to Kulvain's father thinking he had only
to ask and the girl would be his, and he said
unceremoniously,

> "Nganna   wuga."
> "(To) me   give (her)."

But the father replied firmly—

> "Wa   atyu   nginna   wŏmngan."
> "Not   I   (to) you (will) give."

Then Bŏnyī got into a fearful rage and he
said—

> "Wa   nganna   ngindu   wŏmngan   atyu
> "Not   (to) me you   (will) give her,   I
>
>   nginna   wulam dakkērō."
>   you   (will) gash with a knife."

Bŏnyī then slashed away at Kulvain's father,

and that is why the fruit of Kulvain is marked all over with nicks at the present day.

THE SPITEFUL CROW AND THE RESCUE OF THE YOUNG EAGLEHAWK.

(*Kabi Version.*)

A long time ago there was an old Crow that wanted to destroy a young Eaglehawk. So one day when he found the little fellow alone at the camp, he said : " You come here and search my hair for me." But the Eaglehawk said, " No, I won't, there are too many tulum (lice) in it." Then the Crow said angrily : " Hush, hush! don't tell everybody, you make me feel quite ashamed."

When the Crow could not induce him to come near, he called out to him—

"Mŏra,   ngin   wŏnda   tumō,"
"There,   you   climb (that) tree,"

pointing to a little tree near by.

The Eaglehawk was fond of climbing, and being afraid to refuse he began to climb the tree. The Crow kept his eye upon him and as he was climbing he made the tree grow up higher and higher, repeating all the time,

"Tātu, ké, ké, ké, ké,"

until at length the poor little Eaglehawk was so far up that the Crow could barely see him.

While all this was happening, the parents of the Eaglehawk were away in the bush. At last the father said : " I wonder how my little boy is getting on in the camp," and he went back to see if he was all right. The Crow was on the look-out and when he saw the father coming he sneaked away. Then the father searched all round for the little boy but he was nowhere to be found. As he was searching he kept calling out—

" Duwangonga, duwangomalor, manyī, balkarangga."

As he cried out he could hear a faint voice high up replying—

" Yālu,	yālu,	monyuangī
" (My) uncle,	(my) uncle,	about the lice
	guthaangīmoi	yālu."
	was merely pretending	O uncle ! "

The father then gathered all the animals together to see if any one could go up and bring the little fellow down.

There was only one that would venture to do it and that was the Whipsnake. Taking

a dillie-bag with her she climbed the tree.
When she reached the young Eaglehawk she
put him in the dillie-bag and brought him
safely down to the father and mother who
were crying and cutting themselves for grief.
When the young Eaglehawk grew up he
married the Whipsnake.

(*The Wakka Version.*)

There was once an old man who, having
had his dinner, was lying down at the foot of
a tree. A little fellow, his grand-nephew,
was at the top of the same tree, and the old
man cried out to him : " Come down and look
in my head and see if you can find any munyū
(lice)."

The little fellow replied, " No, I won't look
in your head, you're a grey-headed old
man."

Then the old man said : " Go and climb up
that little tree then."

So the boy climbed up a little tree that was
near by and sat on the top of it and the tree
kept growing gradually taller and taller until
the sun went down. It had then grown so

high that the little boy could not get down, and he kept crying out all the time—

    " Yālu   wa,   wa.   Kai   nganya.
    " Uncle (said) climb,   climb.   Here   (am) I.

        Munyūwangē,   kuthawaimai,
        About the lice,   he was merely pretending,
        munyāwangē."
        about the lice."

Next day as he was crying out, two young rosella parrots, who were sisters, came to the place and were chanting—

  " Gilaraan,   gilaraan,   wanya   bundī
  " Head-band,   head-band,   where (is) the water vessel,
              bundī   ngarē."
              the water vessel, ours."

When he heard their voices, he was very glad and cried out louder—

  " Yalō, wa, wa, kai nganya.   Munyūwangē, kuthawaimai,
    munyūwangē."

Then the younger sister said to the older—

        " Ngin   wa   dyauin."
        " You   climb   older sister."

But the older said—

        " Wakka, ngin   wa   kŏnan."
        " No,   you   climb   younger sister."

Then the younger one took the climbing-vine and tried first. Away up and up and up she went till she came to where the tree forked. The fork baffled her, so she came down again and said,

"I couldn't manage it, dyauin."

Then the older one prepared to climb. She took the stone tomahawk and a big dillam (bag) to put the little fellow in, and using the climbing-vine, she went up and up and up till she came to the fork. There she cut two "steps" with the tomahawk and so got above the fork. After that, she easily reached the little boy. She then put him in the dillam and shouted to her sister below—

"You light a fire and cook some dundur (big grubs) and other food to be ready when I get down."

So the younger sister lit a fire and began to cook the dundur. Meanwhile the older one was preparing for coming down. She put the little boy in the dillam, and slung it on her shoulder, she stuck the tomahawk in her girdle, she swung the vine round the tree below the fork, she put her toes in the notches she had cut, and then, stepping backwards and leaning upon the vine, she walked carefully down the tall stem of the tree.

When she took the little boy out of the dillam, she found that he was disgustingly filthy, through neglect, so she told her sister to burn some wood of the iron-bark tree, and make some nguin (charcoal) to paint him with when once she had got him cleaned. She then went to a waterhole, and washed him, and brought him back quite clean. Then she rubbed him all over with powdered charcoal mixed with the fat of the carpet-snake, the way mothers do with their new-born babies. After this was done the sisters sat down and fed him.

Now, all the time that they were handling him, he kept growing bigger and bigger until he had grown to be a young man. When they saw this they asked him : " Shall we be your two wives ? " and he gladly answered " Yes ! "

Then the three of them went towards the camp. He led the way singing—

"Yālu, wa, wa, kai nganya.   Munyūwangē, kutha-
    waimai, munyūwangē,"

and the sisters followed him singing their song—

"Gilaraan, gilaraan, wanya bundī, bundī."

When the brothers in the camp heard the singing they became angry, because they thought someone was mocking their poor lost brother.

At last the oldest brother said : " It's coming closer and closer." It was dark when the lost one came to the camp. He found his mother and all his friends hacking their heads for him till the blood was running down, so great was their mourning.

He came up to them and said—

> " Ngeagŏn."
> " It's I."

Then they began to cry for joy. They spread a 'possum rug on the ground for the two young gins (the rosella parrots) to sit down upon. They all waited on them hand and foot, giving them honey and other kinds of food. They put necklaces of reed beads round their necks and bracelets upon their arms, and made a nice camp for them and the husband they had found.

CHAPTER XII

In the original classification of Australian languages which I give in *Eaglehawk and Crow*, they are divided into six main classes, designated in accordance with the territory over which they were spoken. The third of these classes includes the dialects of New South Wales and those of the south, the centre, and the east of Queensland. It is to subdivision 1 of this third class, embracing the coast languages, that Kabi and Wakka belong.

Being the languages of adjoining tribes, they have a number of words in common, but the surprising fact is the dissimilarity between them both in vocabulary and in inflections. The Kabi language is the more musical, and, to my mind, the least corrupt of the two. The Wakka is more consonantal, it has the palatal ch very decided, and its frequent shorter forms, as compared with Kabi, suggest the operation of a wearing-down process, like what in West Australia has in some instances reduced two words, each originally of two syllables, to a monosyllable.

The pronominal and verbal schemes are more perfectly preserved in Kabi than in Wakka. Kabi, also, more closely resembles the Kamilroi to the south-west than Wakka does.

In Kabi and Wakka there are the same phonic elements and the same order of words in sentences. Both languages are averse to initial vowels, and in both the terminal letters are the liquids, ng or vowels. In both, the sounds of "h" and "s" are foreign.

The distinction between hard and soft mutes is not recognised. The pronunciation of words is not uniform, but varies considerably with different speakers. The difference is conspicuous in certain letters, *e.g.* "t", which, with different speakers, will sound like d, dh, ty, ch or j. Hence the Kabi word for *man* might be written dan, dhan, tan, tyan, chan or jan. It is often difficult to determine the exact quality of a vowel, *e.g.*, whether the word for *where* should be written wanyō or wenyō depends upon the particular speaker, and even with the same person the pronunciation varies.

Other common characteristics are the expression of gender usually by distinct words (an exception being the feminine termination -gan), a liberal use of adverbs compounded with verbs or with verbal indices, the absence of inflections for number in nouns and verbs, and the non-recognition of person in verbs. Another feature is the meagre representation of tense by inflection, adverbs being commonly used to express time.

In the verb, besides terminal inflections, infixes are liberally used, and to a less extent prefixes, to indicate modifications of sense. Threlkeld[1] was, I believe, the first to show how the introduction of a syllable into the heart of a verb delicately varied its meaning. This principle is illustrated in these two languages, and especially in Kabi, as will be shown by examples.

Nouns become adjectives by the addition of such inflections as -nō, -ngur, -dō, -dhau in Kabi and -ngī, -gī in Wakka. Occasionally

[1] *Key to the Struct. of the Abor. Lang.*

nouns and adjectives and frequently adverbs
became transformed into verbs by suffixing a
verbal determinant. Examples are :—

> nguyum, *sweat*, nguyum-bŏman, *to perspire*,
> kunna, *neck*, kunna-mara, *to wring the neck*,
> yīkī, *the same*, *likewise*, yīkī-man, *to resemble*,
> kurī, *around*, kurī-man, *to revolve*.

In simple sentences the order is subject,
indirect object, object, adverb, verb. The
adjective follows the noun it qualifies. Modify-
ing phrases and conditional clauses usually
come first in compound sentences. Prohibitive
sentences, in Kabi, are introduced by the
negative adverb " bar." It should, however,
be observed that the structure of sentences
admits of considerable flexibility.

Mental states are usually expressed by words
or phrases descriptive of some physical action
or condition. Examples are :—

> Nŏlla kalangur (lit. stomach or inside, good),
>   *cheerful*,
> Nŏlla warabin (inside trembling), *frightened*,
> Nŏlla kaiyaman (inside biting), *sorry*,
> Mī kambīman (eyes hiding), *jealous*,
> Murū wŏmbalīman (nose uplifting), *supercilious*,
> Pīnang baluman (ears dying), *to forget*.

M

Nouns and adjectives are frequently conjoined to express one idea, thus :—

Kaiwun kabī (desire wanting), means *lazy*,
Pīnang gulūm (ears dull), means *deaf* or *mad*.

THE KABI LANGUAGE

PHONIC ELEMENTS

Vowels

	a ā	o (as in Eng. ton)	â (as in warm)
e (as in Eng. yet)	e ē	o ō	
	i ī	u ū	

Diphthongs

au ai iu oi ou ua ui

Consonants

k g ng
t d th dh ty (almost like palatal ch) y r rr (muffled cerebral)
l n ñ (ny) ndh
p b v w m

VALUE OF THE LETTERS

The following values apply to the spelling in both Kabi and Wakka—

a	as in Eng.	bath
ā	,,	far
ĕ	,,	yet, her
e	,,	pen
ē	,,	ei in rein
i	,,	pin
ī	,,	ravine
ŏ	,,	son

â as in Eng. warm
o   ,,   on
ō   ,,   lone
u   ,,   full
ū   ,,   oo in food
au as in Lat. causa and ou in Eng. pound
ai as i in Eng. wine
ou as ow in Eng. mown nearly
ng as in Eng. sing
nng   ,,   finger
nng   ,,   pruning with i omitted
ny   ,,   Span. ñ

The hard and soft consonants are not consistently distinguished, in fact the distinction is practically non-existent.

Neither l nor r occurs initially. The terminal sounds are the liquids, ng, ndh and vowels. Initial vowels occur but rarely. Such combinations as pr kr are sometimes used at the beginning of a syllable, but between the consonants a semi-vowel steals in. S is found only in the dog-call "isē," which is probably a Papuan or Melanesian word. H only occurs in one or two foreign words. Not only are the dentals t, d, interchangeable, but they may take the form of dh or ty or even of clear palatal ch with some speakers. This remark holds good for most if not for all Australian dialects. The sound which I have represented by dh is that which would be produced by a sound of d preceding and coalescing with th in English *that*. V is the equivalent of b with some speakers. Thus, " vrŏngaman," *to hear*, is pronounced in some parts " brangaman." It is difficult to determine what the initial consonant in this word originally was, as the stem seems to be identical with the Victorian word " wirng," the *ear*.

A feature of Kabi common to Australian languages and also to Tasmanian is the elision of the letter g (or k) where it occurs between two vowels. Thus " buga " or " bua," *foul smell;* " bugaman " or " baman," *to come;* compare S. Australian Buandik for Bugandaity, the name of a tribe, and Tasmanian " pah " for " pugga," *a man*. In Australian dialects there is a similar elision of the letter r.

Reduplication is common. Where letters are doubled each requires to be distinctly heard.

The same spelling has not been invariably adhered to for the same word, the reason being that the pronunciation, even of common words, is slightly varied by different speakers, and the pronunciation of the one individual is not always consistent.

THE NOUN.

Although there is no article consciously employed, yet it seems to me that there was in the original Papuasian speech a substantival index or determinant with the force of an article, well marked in the Tasmanian -na. The trace of this article, or noun-index, is observable in the nouns which are most widely distributed in Australia, such as dīn-na, *foot*, tulla-na, *tongue*, pin-na, *ear*. Sometimes it is only represented by the letter n. In Kabi this primitive ending is usually represented by -nang or -ning, *e.g.*, pī-nang, *ear*, ki-ning, *arm*, gu-nang, *excrement*. Probably this terminal index in Tasmanian and Australian nouns corresponds to the so-called article na-, which is initial in Melanesian.

Plurality is denoted, not by inflection, but by an adjective added, thus, "dhu," *tree*, "dhu bŏnggan,". *tree many*, or *trees*. Gender is not regularly distinguished by inflection, but some proper names of females and a few common names take -kan or -gan as a feminine termination. This is the case with the class-names, *e.g.*, Bŏnda, fem. Bŏnda-gan, and correlative terms such as "nyulang," the relationship existing between son-in-law and mother-in-law, the feminine form being "nyulang-gan." Similarly, "kanī" means *son*, "kanī-gan," *daughter*. But usually the equivalents of *man, woman, father, mother*, are employed to mark the sex.

Declension

Case, or what corresponds to case, is expressed by numerous terminations, a few of them occurring with great frequency. The simple stem is used both for the nom. and acc., but -na or -nga usually marks the acc. case, and sometimes even the nom. There is also a special form for the subject when it is nominative to a verb of action, and especially to an active, transitive verb, as is general in Australian languages.

The subjoined paradigm exhibits the most common inflections.

Nom. simple the stem alone or with -na added as yĕramin, *horse.*

,,   agent -dō or -rō, as yĕramin-dō, *horse*, dhakkē-rō, *a stone.*

Gen.	-nō or -ū, as	yĕramin,-nō	kung-ū, *of the water.*
Dat. to or into	-nō		nŏlla-nō, *to the hole.*
,, to go for	-gō	yĕramin-gō	kung-gō, *for water.*
Acc.	-na	yĕramin-na	nguin-na, *the boy*(obj.).
Abl.	-nī		nŏlla-nī, *in the hole.*
,, because of	-karī	yĕramin-karī	
,, along with, upon	,,	,,	wabun - gari, *on the stump.*
,, instrument	-rō		kuthar-rō, *with a club.*

Other illustrations are—

> ngurūin-nī, *by day.*
> kīra-mī, *at the fire.*
> kīra-ba, *with or in the fire.*
> nīrīm-ba, *in the middle.*

The termination -gō is used both with nouns and verbs, thus, dhurī-gō bam-gō yan-gō, *to-the-scrub for-eggs going.* It sometimes means *motion to*, sometimes *purpose*, being, in the latter case, equivalent to English *for.* Another peculiarity is the frequent use of -nga as an affix to any part of speech. It is an accusative ending and also a copulative conjunction, but it often occurs in an untranslatable way, as, for instance, "Tangka-nga Tommy-nga"—"*(Say) Thank you (to) Tommy.*"

PRONOUN

The personal pronoun is richly inflected by case-endings, but is not inflected for distinction of number, unless we are to suppose that the termination -lī, in first person plural has the significance of plurality, which is probable. Gender is undistinguished phonically. The personal pronoun is a typical Australian example of this part of speech.

PARADIGM OF PERSONAL PRONOUN

SINGULAR   PLURAL

First Person

Nom. (simple) I, ngai   We,   ngal'ī, ngal'īn
„   (agent) „ nga'dhū *or* a'tyū „   ngal'indō
Poss. My, Mine ngan'yunggai Our, Ours, ngal'īnngur ngal'-
                                                  īnnō
Dat. Me,   ngai'bŏla   Us,   ngal'īn-gō
Acc. „   ngan'na   „   ngal'īn

Second Person

Nom. (simple) Thou, ngin   You,   ngul'am
„   (emphatic) „   ngin'dai, ngin'bilin
„   (agent)   „   ngin'dū
Poss. Thy, Thine, ngin'yŏnggai   Your, Yours, ngul'-
                                                  amō
Dat. Thee,   ngin'bŏla, ngin'bangō You,   ngul'-
                                                  ambŏla
Acc. „   ngin'na

                  Nom. You all,   ngu'pū
                  Poss. Yours,   ngu'punū
                  Acc. You all,   ngu'punga

Third Person

Nom. (simple) He, She, It, ngun'da   They, dhin'abū
„   (agent) „   „   ngun'darō   „   dhina'burō

Language

Poss. His, Her, Hers, Its, ngun'danō Their, Theirs, dhina'-
                                                 bunō
Dat. Him, Her, It,   ngun'dabŏla Them, dhina'bubŏla,
                                          dhina'bunga
Acc.   „   „   ngun'danō   „   dhin'abunga

DUAL

Inclusive, 2nd and 1st persons, Thou and I, ngal'īnngin (lit.
                                                 we thou)
Exclusive, 3rd and 1st persons, Another and I, ngŏl'ŏm
                   2nd person, You two,   bul'la
                   3rd person, They two, bul'la

As in other Australian languages, the Relative
Pronoun is lacking.

INDEFINITE PRONOUNS

Anyone, Everyone, Everybody,   kar'vandhī'lum
Everyone,   kŏm'kalim

USED WITH PERSONAL PRONOUNS SINGULAR AND PLURAL

    Self,   mit'dhī
    By oneself,   mit'dhīnō

PRONOMINAL ADJECTIVES

    Another's,   dhŏm'kaiyīr
    Other,   kar'va
    Some . . . Others   kar'va . . . kar'va
    This one   ka'ringa
    That one   kŏr'adhū

The adverb " karī," pronounced also " kathī "
and " kaī," is the stem of several of the above

forms. The termination -va is also pronounced ba, in which form it is widely current to change the adverb into numerals and pronouns. For demonstrative, the third personal is used, and also the pronominal adjectives "ka'ringa," this one, and "kŏradhu," that one.

INTERROGATIVE PRONOUNS

Nom. (simple)	Who	ngan'gai
,, (agent)	,,	ngan'dō
Poss.	Whose	ngan'yunggai
Dat.	Whom	ngan'gaibŏla
Dat. and Acc.	Whom	ngā'na, ngan'gaiminī
Nom. (simple)	What	min'yanggai
,, (agent)	,,	ngan'dō
	What is the matter?	wan'duroman

Demonstrative and Indefinite Pronouns are subject to inflection by suffixes like the Noun. Two of these suffixes -pa and -na, it is interesting to notice, as they are virtually of universal occurrence in Australian languages. The first where it occurs in Kabi has become inseparable from the stem, as, for instance, in "kar-va," or "kar-ba," *another*.

The root "kar" is no doubt the same as in the adverb "karī," *here ;* -ba added makes it a demonstrative, which can be used as a sub-

stantive and then the word can take the postfix
-na, which we have seen is primarily a nounal
index. Variants of this word "karba" occur
very widely for the numeral *one* in such forms
as kur-na, kuri-pa, kutu-pŏna.

THE ADJECTIVE, ADVERB AND CONJUNCTION

Adjectives generally are not distinguishable
from nouns by peculiarity of form. There are,
however, many exceptions, chiefly in the case of
adjectives formed from nouns by the addition
of an adjectival termination. The most
common of these is -ngur (sometimes -ngū or
nō) the genitive sign in pronouns, which can
be suffixed to nouns to imply the possession of
the quality expressed by the noun, as wulwī,
smoke, wulwī-ngur, *smoky*, dhilīl, *noise*, dhilīl-
ngur, *noisy*, bŏkka, *horn*, bŏkka-ngur, *horned*.
The same termination is sometimes added to
an adjective and appears to slightly vary the
sense, thus, kŏnan, *kind*, kŏnan-ngur, *quiet*,
tame, unfortunate ; baiyī, *sore*, baiyī-ngur, *sick*.
This suffix occurs in Kamilroi to mark the
possessive case of nouns and is the sign of the
same case in the Kabi pronoun, 1st person
plural.

Another adjectival ending is -dhau or -dō, *e.g.*, wuin, *night*, wuin-dhau, *dark*, buran, *wind*, buran-dō, *windy*.

Still another such ending is -ban or -bandh, varied to -wan, -wen or -wendh. It is suffixed to nouns, adjectives or adverbs. Examples are wuru, *before*, wuru-wendh, *old;* dhandar, *slippery*, dhandar-ban, *agreeable;* dhalī, *now*, dhalī-ban, *new*.

The adjective, when used as such, is not declined. It is generally compared by the help of adverbs like "karba" (or "karva") *very*. Another mode of comparison is to say of an object, this is large, this is good, and so forth, a comparison with other objects being implicit.

The adverb has no distinguishing phonic index. It occasionally has the adjectival ending -ngur. Adverbs in -ni and -na may be regarded also as locative cases of nouns. Common nominal suffixes are joined to adverbs and modify their meaning, *e.g.*, "bīya," *back*, "bīya-ni," *at the back*; wurū, *out, first*, "wurū-nī," *at the front before*.

Conjunctions are very sparingly used. The commonest are "wenyō, *if*, "bŏn'na," *when*, 'nga," *and*. The first two are used rather to modify than to conjoin. Judging from conversations I have heard, I am of opinion that a phrase was often joined to the one following by hanging on to the final letter of the first.

Interrogative Words

The stems " min " (or " minya ") and " wen " (or " wenyō) take on numerous suffixes. The first of these has a counterpart in the Malay " man," the second in the Melanesian " ua," " ue," " uan," and the Tasmanian " wana."

mina′nī	why
mina′lō	,,
minya′ma	how many
minya′nū	what place
min′yanggō	how
(min′yanggai	what, Inter. Pron.)
wen′ya, wen′dyō, or wen′yō	where
wen′yōminī	wherever
wen′yō	when
wen′yōbŏla	when (at what time)
wen′yarī	how getting on
wan′yiram	which way
wen′yiragō	whatever
,,	wherever
wan′dyuramathī	how is it
wan′dhurathin	why

Numerals.

The numeral system is binary. To express a number higher than two the terms for one and two are combined as may be necessary. " Kālim " or " kualim," *one*, " bulla," *two*, " bulla kālim," *three*, " bulla bulla," or " bulla kira bulla," *four*. The enumeration may be conducted higher after the same manner, but generally numbers above four are expressed by "gurwinda" or "bŏnggan," many.

THE VERB

The verb has various forms, as *Simple, Reciprocal, Causative, Intensive.* But, in certain instances, what might be regarded as a special form might equally be regarded as a distinct derivative from the simple form. Infinitive, Indicative, Purposive, Suppositional and Imperative moods are distinguishable with well-marked terminations. The infinitive and indicative may, however, be said to overlap. Tense as indicated by termination is very wavering, the same forms serving on occasions for present, past, and future time. There is a clearly-marked preterite, terminating in "n," which serves also as a perfect participle and does duty for a passive voice which otherwise is wanting. The infinitive is employed as an imperfect participle, and there is also a verbal noun.

The shortest and simplest form is the imperative. Often it is one syllable, it rarely exceeds two, but sometimes adds "-mŏrai." Its termination is always in vowel sounds.

The general verbal notion is expressed by the infinitive index, which is usually "-man," "-mathī," or "-thin." Some verbs have an infinitive in two of these endings, thus there is "yanman" and "yanmathī," *to go*, "nyindaman" and "nyindathin," *to enter*. The difference between the significance of "-man" and "-mathī" is slight, if any, but as compared with "-thin" the two former indicate more commonly *state* or *inactivity*, the latter *action* or *motion*. What I have called the Purposive Mood has the termination "-thin" for its index, but as verbs with this ending do not invariably denote purpose, it must be taken also occasionally for the sign of the infinitive. For instance, "yaman" and "yamathī," from stem "ya," alike mean *to speak*, but "ya-thin" means *wish to speak, purpose speaking*, thus

"Yakoi! atyu nginna yathin," means "Come here, I want to speak to you."

Person is not distinguished by sound, but has either to be inferred, or the pronoun is expressed and precedes the verb. Conjugation is by prefixes, affixes, and infixes. The prefixes are usually of adverbial force, the affixes impart the modal, temporal and participial signification, and the infixes may be regarded as possessing *formal* power, expressing generally causative and intensive variations of the sense, only it should be observed that the index of the reciprocal *form* is terminal.

The following exemplify the use of prefixes—

> bīya-bŏman, *to come back*, from bīya, *back*, baman (or bŏkaman) *to come ;*
> yīkī-yaman, *to answer*, from yīkī, *the same, likewise*, yaman, *to speak ;*
> wurū-bŏman, *to come out*, from wurū, *out*, baman *to come ;*
> yīvarī, *to put, to make*, is probably derived from "barī," *to bring,*
> and is varied to mīvarī, *to put away*, and to wuruyīvari- thinī, *to put out.*
> In "bī-wathin," *to play*, "wathin," means *to laugh*, and "bī-" is an intensifying preformative; in "bī-

yelī," *to cooey*, "yelī" means *to shout*, and "bī-"
has an intensifying or prolonging force. In "bī-
dha-līn-da," to cause *to drink*, the initial syllable
transforms the Simple into the Causative Form,
or rather helps to do so, for "-lī" and "da" are
also concerned in the change, "dhathin" being
the vocable meaning *to drink*.

The following are examples of affixes :—

"-man," "-mathī," "-thin," regular signs of infinitive,
  of imperfect indicative, and imperfect participle ;
"-an," "-in," "-un," signs of preterite, perfect participle and passive sense ;
"-ra," "-thin," "-thinī," futurity, purpose, and possi-
  bility ;
"-ei," "-ba," "-da," "-ga," "-na," "-nga," "-ngai,"
  marks of imperative mood ;
"-aio," "-aü," distinguish the suppositional mood ;
"-na," "-ba," are signs of the gerundive and imperfect
  participle ;
"-ira" has the sense of forcing or pressing ;
"-iu" implies irregular movement, as exemplified in
  "kauwaliu," *to search ;* "maliu," *to change ;* "yan-
  diriu," *to perambulate ;*
"-mathin," "-bathin," "-wathin," transform other
  parts of speech into verbs and impart the signi-
  fications respectively of (1) *purpose*, (2) *becoming*,
  (3) *holding* or *making :*
"-yulaiyu" is the index of the Reciprocal Form, *e.g.*,
  "baiyī," *to strike ;* "baiyulaiyu," *to fight, i.e., to
  strike one other ;* "ya," *speak ;* "yathulaiyu," *to
  converse, etc.*

N

Infixes. — Such terminations as "-man," "-mathī" express the general verbal sense, having some such force as *do* or *make*. Without removing this general verbal sign, one or more syllables may be interposed between it and the stem; this is the usual mode of indicating the Causative and Intensive Forms.

"Karī" means *here* or *in;* "karimī" (for "kari-mathī") is *to enter*, with preterite "karin." There is also a verb "karī-na-man," and another "karīn-di-mī," both meaning *to put in;* "-na-" and "-di-" are the causative indices. "Dungī-man" means *to cry;* "dungī-nura-man" *to make to cry;* "kurī-gō" is *to turn round;* "kurī-man" *to revolve;* "kurī-na-man" *to cause to turn;* "kurī-mathin-da" also *to cause to turn*, so that in these examples "-nura-," "-na-" and final "-da" mark the Causative Form.

The word "buwandīman" means *to herd*, lit. *to cause to stop;* it is thus compounded "buwan," *to stand*, "-di-" causative sign, "-man," verbal sign.

The inflex "-lī-" is introduced to imply doing well, progress, advantage. The following are examples :—There is a stem "yangga," having the meaning of *making.* The ordinary infinitive is "yanggō-man," *to make;* "yangga-lī-thin" is *to make well, to cure;* "yangga-lī-nō-man" is *to allow,* from "yangga-," "-li-," *to advantage;* "-nō-," *permission;* "-man," the verbal sign. "Wŏmba" is the imperative meaning, *lift;* "wŏmba-lī-man," *to fall upon;* "wŏmba-lin," *carrying;* the word "wŏmba-li-mar-aio" may therefore be thus analysed, "wŏmba-," *to lift;* "-li-," *motion;* "-mar-," sign of futurity, "-aio," mark indicating supposition.

One kind of modification yet remains to be noted—viz., reduplication. This is the usual sign of the Intensive Form, *e.g.,* "yĕlīman," *to shout;* "yĕlī-yĕlī-man," *to speak quickly;* "dhŏman," *to eat;* "dhan-dhŏman," *to gnaw;* "dhŏmma" means *to catch;* "dhŏmma-thin," *to hold, to grip;* "dhŏmma-man," *to marry, i.e.,* to catch and hold fast.

GRAMMATICAL NOTES ON WAKKA

My notice of the grammar of Wakka will be brief, as I have not the same command of this language as I have of Kabi. The observations given here will, however, be found correct, I think, as far as they go. Many of the remarks already made upon Kabi apply equally to Wakka.

THE NOUN

The distinction of number is not indicated by inflection but by the addition of an adjective. As in Kabi, a feminine suffix -gan (or -kan) is attached to a very few masculine or common names. This suffix may be just a variant of "gin" (g hard) the term for woman. When gender is to be indicated without this suffix some adjective is used to specify the sex. We have seen that in Kabi "malimgan," *wife*, is the feminine of a rare term "malim," *husband*, so in Wakka "nyōm," *husband*, has a feminine "nyōm-gan." Jŏnjarin-gan is the feminine of Jŏnjarī, the name of a beneficent supernatural being.

The case relations are expressed both by terminal inflection and by the use of separate words immediately preceding the noun. What may be called case-endings seem to be fewer in Wakka than in Kabi.

The commonest suffix is -nī, varied to -ī. Examples are "kundu," *bark*, "kundu-nī," *on the bark*, "kung," *water*, "kung-ī" *in the water.* The suffix -man signifies *belonging to, related to, possessing,* e.g., "kulībŏra-mana," *belonging to the* "kulībŏra" (*honeycomb people*), "jŏnjari-man," *befriended by* or *possessing* "Jŏnjarī." A suffix "-wangē" has the meaning *concerning.*

THE PRONOUN

	SINGULAR	PLURAL
	First Person	
Nom. (simple) I	ngia	nga'īnga
„ (agent) „	a'tyu	
Poss. My, Mine	nga'rī	nga'īra
Acc. Me	ngon'ya	nga'īna

In the plural a medial "1" has evidently been elided.

	Second Person	
Nom. (simple) Thou	ngin	ngū
„ (agent) „	ngin'du	
Poss. Thy, Thine	ngin'gorī	ngū'rīa
Acc. Thee	ngin'na	ngū'na

	Third Person		
Nom. He, She, It	yoa, moa		gŏ'na
Poss. His, Her, Hers, Its	yong'garī,	yo'rī	yau'rī
Acc. Him, Her, It	mŏn'na		yau'na

	Dual
Nom. We two	ngam'ngin
Poss. Our, Ours	ngam'garī
Acc. Us two	ngam'a

	Pronominal Adjectives
Nom. That one	kŏr'ai, mŏr'a
Poss. That one's	kŏr'arī, mŏr'arī

INTERROGATIVE PRONOUNS

Who	ngan'unda
What	ngan'dō, nyan'da

(What is it ? nyan'dī ī'ngī)

THE ADJECTIVE, ADVERB AND CONJUNCTION.

There is no article. The adjective is not inflected. There are a few adjectival terminations, the commonest being -ngī, varied to -gī, otherwise the adjective is undistinguishable from the noun.

The adverb is likewise undistinguishable from the noun in form.

The copulative conjunction is usually "nga," as in Kabi, another word similarly used is "gŏn'a."

NUMERALS

One	ka'buin
Two	boi'yō
Three	kor'omda
Many	mai'yan

INTERROGATIVE WORDS

how	wan'darumau
,,	win'yuramau
how many	nyam'ma
why	nan'gō
where	wĕn'yō, wĕn

when	wen'yuala
,,	wen'yamga
what is the matter ?	wan'daran-ga
why	nan'gō

THE VERB

The verb appears to be very simple in its conjugation. It has neither person nor number. There is a past tense which is also the perfect participle. It has Forms, *Simple*, *Reciprocal*, *Causative*, and *Intensive*, as in Kabi, it also has Moods.

The imperative is the stem. The perfect participle usually ends in " -ai." The suffix " -jau " marks the Reciprocal Form, " -jinga " the Intensive, and " -ndī," or " -dī," the Causative.

The following examples will illustrate the above remarks :—

"Bea," *come*, imperative mood, "ba," infinitive, "bai," past tense and perfect participle.

" Ya," *speak*, imperative and infinitive, "yai," past tense and perfect participle.

" Bi'yanga," *to hear*, infinitive, " bi'yangai," past tense and perfect participle.

" Bu'ma," *strike*, imperative, "bum'bē," infinitive, " bum'jau," Reciprocal Form, " bum'jinga," *to kill*, Intensive Form.

"Jia," *to run*, infinitive and imperative, "jen'dī" *to make to run*, Causative Form.

The suffix "-gŏn" joined to a noun or pronoun supplies the place of the verb *to be e.g.*, "ngia-gŏn," *It is I*. The substantive verb is often implied in the pronoun or demonstrative word, as "mŏn'kungī," *it (is) in the water*.

VOCABULARY

NOUNS

MAN AND HIS RELATIONSHIPS

English	Kabi	Wakka
Aunt, father's sister	yu'ruin	kŏm'mī
„ mother's sister	a'vang *or* nga'bang	ngŏn'yan
Baby	wŏl'bai	nyu'ni nyu'ni
Blackfellow	dhan *or* tyan	mu'ran
Blackwoman	yī'ran *or* yīr'kan	gin (g hard) bō' varin
Boy	nguin	ba'rang ba'rang
Brother, elder	nun	tyatya
„ younger	wu'thung	chuan *or* dyu'ang
Coast blacks	bī'dhala	ba'tyala
Child	wŏl'bai	nyu'ni nyu'ni, non'na
Daughter	kan'ingan, dŏran'-angan	nyu'na
Daughter-in-law	kŏlanmīn	
Father	pa'bun	ba'bu
Father-in-law	kŏm'mī	
Girl	wu'ru *or* wur'gu	gin (g hard)
Grandfather, paternal	mai'bīn	meī
„ maternal	nga'thang	ngat'ya
Grandmother, paternal	kŏm'arŏm	wai'yu, we'andam
„ maternal	yĕn'an	bu'iya
Husband	mal'lim, ma'lith-anmī	nyōm
„	dhan'dōr	

225

ENGLISH	KABI	WAKKA
Inland blacks	wa'pa	
Man, adult	kī'var	kī'par
„ old	win'yir	ku'rīlnga
Mother	a'vang *or* nga'bang	ngŏn'yan
Mother-in-law	nyu'langgan	
Nephew, sister's son	ka'nī, bu'ranyin	
„ brother's son	ka'ni	
Niece, sister's daughter	ka'ningan	
„ brother's daughter	„	
Sister, elder	ya'bun	ja'wuin *or* dyau'in
„ younger	nai'bar	kŏn'dan
Son	ka'ni, nu'kīvar	
Son-in-law	nyu'lang, ku'tha-rum	
Uncle, father's brother	pa'bun	ba'bu
„ mother's brother	kŏm'mī	ma'ma
White man	mŏth'ar, dhī	
„ woman	dha'ran	
Widow	ku'lun	
Widower	bu'rong, bu'rŏn-dŏm	
Wife	ma'līm-gan, ma'-līmīn-gan	nyōm-gan
Woman	yī'ran	gin (g hard)
„ old	ma'run	

PARTS OF THE BODY

English	Kabi	Wakka
Ankle		wu'lu
Arm	kin'ing	kin'ing
Armpit		wam'gīr
Back	bun'dhur	bu'rum, dhē
Belly	dhu'ngun	mu
Beard	yĕr'an	yik'ka

Vocabulary

ENGLISH	KABI	WAKKA
Blood	kak′kē	dīr
Bone	ngīm	gī′ra
Bowels	gu′nang	ku′nang
Breast	dhan′dar	dhan′dar
Breasts	a′mŏng	nga′mung
Breath	ngai′ya	kun′bīr
Calf of leg	bu′yu	bu′yu
Cheek	wang′gum	wang′ga
Chest	dhan′dar	tŏn′dar
Chin	yīk′kal	yīk′ka
Collar-bone	ku′ru	gung gung
Ear	pī′nang	pī′nang
Elbow	kun′dī	ku′lumur, ku′lumbul
Eyebrow	ting′gur	dhip′īn
Eyelash	dhī′pindyin	bu′el bu′el
Eye	mī	ma
Face	ngu	ngwar
Fat	ma′ron	
Finger	mŏl′la	na
Finger-nail	mŏl′la, gillen	gil′īn
Foot	dhī′nang	chi′nang, dyī′nang
Forehead	nyun′gal	ngu′wa
Generative organ, female	nŏl′la	
Hair	dhil′la	gam
Hand	pī′rī	na
Head	kaṁ	mau
Heart	tuk′kū	
Hip		mun
Hip-joint		ka′nīm
Hocks	yil′la	
Inside	nŏl′lanī	
Knee	dhī′mī	bun′dur
Leg	tĕr′ang	
Lip	dham′bur	tam′bur

ENGLISH	KABI	WAKKA
Liver	kŏn'ang	
Loins	ngam'am	
Lung	wang	
Milk	a'mŏng	
Mouth	tang'ka	dī'ang
Nape of the neck	kun'na	wan'dar
Neck	,,	
Nose	mu'rū	mī
Penis	dhun	
Phlegm	bun'yu	
Rib	ku	
Rump	mu'mū	
Shoulder	ngil'kī	
Shoulder-blade		bŏ'tang
Sinew	ku'kīn	kai'ang
Skin	ku'bar	dŏ'mē, pa'ru pa'ru
Stomach	dhu'ngun	mu
Sweat	ngu'yūm	
Tears	ngi'yul	ngwol
Teeth	tang'ka	dī'ang
Thigh	tĕr'ang	tyo'ngar
Throat	yīp'pī	
Toe	pī'rī dhī'nang	
Tongue	tu'nam	tu'nam
Urine	ka'bur	ka'bur
Vein	kak'kē	
Whiskers	yĕr'an	

NAMES OF QUADRUPEDS, ETC.

Animal (generic name)	mu'rang	ni'yang
Bandicoot	dhun'kal	bī'nur, bō'andh
Bat	ngū'leyam	dyu'gur
Bear, native	kul'la	gul'la
Cat, native	yu'ruthūn	īn'dyun

ENGLISH	KABI	WAKKA
Dingo	wĕt'ya ka'rum	wā'tya
Dog, domestic	wĕt'ya	bu'gin, bu'gin kunang'anan
Dugong	yu'angan	
Flying fox, large bat	gī'raman	
Horse	yĕr'aman	
Kangaroo	ma'rī	ko'rōman
„ old man	ku'rūman	
„ female	yī'mar	
„ rat	pai	ba'rungga
Opossum, grey	ngaram'bī, kurū'ī	jo'wan
Paddimelon	bwal, bu'gal	mid'den
Platypus	dhur'kū	
Porcupine (echidna)	kak'kar	kar
Squirrel, flying	mu'bīr, bang'kū	
Wallaby	wovar'ngur	wai'ya
„ rock	wŏl'lan	

NAMES OF BIRDS

Bird	dhip'pī	jui, kun'yur
Bustard, forest turkey	kalar'ka	ka'gora
Cockatoo, black	dha'rukal, geyam'-biau, wīy'al	cho'rō, dha'ra
„ white	gig'um	kēr
Crane	yī'laibōdhŏ'man	yī'līthē
Crow	wō'wa	wō'wa
Duck, black	nar	ngyēm
„ wood-duck		mō'narong
Eaglehawk	bu'thar	ngai'yel
Eagle, white-hooded	kang'ka	
Emu	ngu'ruin	nguī
Fantail, shepherd's companion	dhing'ka dhing'ka	
Hawk, large brown	til'gonda	

ENGLISH	KABI	WAKKA
Hawk, streaked	min min	
Ibis	mu'rūgū'ran	bun'dur
Laughing jackass	ka'wung	ku'garka
Magpie (Shrike)	ku'rumbūl	
„ Lark	din'da	
Mallee Hen or Scrub Turkey	wa'wun	
Native Companion		ma'guī
Owl	ing'ka	
Parrakeet (Green Leek)	pīr	
Pelican	gul'uin	jun'gar
Pigeon, Wonga	wongga'laman	wung
„ Bronzewing	mam	
Rail, Water	dha'ran, dhīm	
Swan, Black	ku'lūn	ku'loin
Teal	dhu'bun	tyin'onggir
Water-hen, (Porphyrio)	wa'thom	
Woodpecker, native	yin'dīrīn	
Wren, Blue Bonnet, etc.	dhu'runkalīm	

FISHES

Catfish	ba'la	ba'la
Codfish	tu'kū	
Crayfish	yīl'lai	yīl
Lobster		„
Minnow	bu'rūn	
Mullet	ngŏndai'ya	ngan'de
„ small	dhu'ra	

REPTILES

Frog	wŏr'ba	
Iguana	wa'ruī	chun'ban
Lizard, Jew	pī'nang gŏr'an	

ENGLISH	KABI	WAKKA
Lizard, Sleepy	wundum	
„ Water	wa'ran	
Scorpion	yī'lai	
Snake (generic)	mu'rang (animal)	yu'win
„ Black	mul'lu	
„ Brown	mu'rūgī'rai	
„ Carpet	wŏng'ai	yu'win
„ Deaf Adder	mun'dulum	
„ Diamond	kīp'pa	
„ Grey	yil'lam	
„ Short	gu'lūm	
„ Spotted Scrub	dhīwan'tī	
„ Whip	yi'yun, ngun'dar	
„ Yellow	mu'rai	
Turtle, Fresh-water	mībīr	

INSECTS

Ant, common, small	king, mon'dhūr	mon'dhūr, bo'-raom
„ Jumper	ba'riya	beng'ga
„ small black	ba'rŏm	bu'amben
„ Soldier	mum'ba	bēng'gamōnin
„ White	nga'rī	ko'nōr
Bee, native dark	gīl'la	kat'ya
„ grey	ka'vai	goi'yē, kē
Butterfly	ba'lumbīr	
Centipede	kī'rai	nyīr
Fly	dhip'pī	dīng
Grub, large edible	bu'rūga	dun'dur
Hornet, large	kau'war	
„ small	yau'wa	
Louse	tu'lum	mun'yū
Mosquito	min'yīr, bun'ba	
Scorpion	yī'lai	
Spider	mŏth'ar	
Worm	ku'laren	jīm

NAMES OF PLANTS

English	Kabi	Wakka
Cunjevoi (a manioc-like plant)	yim'bun	
Grass	ban	ban
Moss	wu'bung	
Punk, woody fungus	pa'bunba're	
Raspberry, native	mal'kalang	mu'numu'nomba
Sarsaparilla (plant so called)	bor'abor'andin	
Scrub Berry, small	kun'dīlam	pun'dungga
,, Plum	kul'vain	
Tree	dhū	dha'dhū
,, Apple, native	bu'pū	
,, Bastard Box	dhin'kar	
,, Black Butt	dhu'lar	
,, Bloodwood	bū'nar	
,, Blue Gum	yir'ra	man'burar
,, Bottle	bī'rimgan	
,, Box	min'ka	buar'ngan
,, Bunya	bŏn'yī	
,, Cabbage	ka'wa	
,, Cabbage Palm	pī'bīn	
,, Cedar	wut'dha	
,, Cherry, native	bir'ra bir'ra	
,, Currajong	ka'yan, kun'marim	
,, Cyprus Pine	ku'loloi	
,, Dogwood	mam'bū	
,, Grass	tok'ka	chak'ke
,, Honeysuckle, native	bŏth'arŏm	
,, Iron-bark, narrow-leafed	du'būn	bai'ī
,, Iron-bark, broad-leafed	bul'yel	keg'er
,, Ironwood	nan'garin	

ENGLISH	KABI	WAKKA
Tree, Moreton Bay Ash	ku'randūr	
„ Oak (Silky) (*Grevillea*)	yul'lō	
„ Oak (Swamp)	bīl'lai	
„ Pine	kū'nyam	
„ Plum (Scrub)	kul'vain	
„ Red Gum	dhom'ba	
„ Stinging	gim'pī	
„ Stringybark	dhu'wai	
„ Tea (*Melaleuca*)	nam'būr	
„ Wattle, Black	dhīl'gar	
„ „ Green	bu'pīn	
Vine, *Flagellaria Indica*	yur'rū	

INANIMATE NATURE

Bank	kun'na	tan'dan
Bush, the	bamp'pī	
Cloud	mŏn'dam	bel, ku'ruī
Country	dha *or* tya	chaun
Creek	wir'ra	du'ngīr, kī'rar
Darkness	muin	ngun'yun
Day	ngu'rūindhau	ngu'nar
Daylight	dhu'luru, bar'bīman	git'tī, git'tībē
Earth	dha *or* tya	cha
Fire	kī'ra	kui'yum
Flat, a	bīr'rū	wan
Flood	ngum'ma	dyōn
Frost	pī'ringga	
Gully	dhĕr'ang	
Hole	nŏl'la	nŏl'la
Light	ngu'ruin	git'tī
Lightning	bŏl'la	mŏr'ra
Mist	ku'ang	dam, ku'ang
Mountain	tun'ba, kun'da	bu'rū

o

ENGLISH	KABI	WAKKA
Moon	ba'pun	gu'lauwa
Mud	dhil'ang	
Night	wuin'dhau	ngun'yun
Quartz	kung'kam	
Rain	yu'rūng	ku'wong
Rainbow	dhak'kan	gyau'war
Ridge	kun'da	
Sea	ting'īra	
Shadow	ngū'thurū	ngul
Sky	ngu'rūindh	ngu'nar
Smoke	wul'wī	jum
Star	kal'bar	ku'gī
Stone	dhak'kē	dai
Summit	ba'ringa	
Sun	ngu'rūindh, tī'rum	ji'gam
Sundown	tī'rum ka'rīn	
Sunrise	tī'rum wŏn'dan	
Thunder	mum'ba	mi're
Twilight	buin mul'lū, mul'- lūbon	
Water	kung	kung
Watershed	nuk'ku	
Wind	bu'ran	bu'ran
Wood	dhū	dha'dhū

MANUFACTURED ARTICLES

Bag	bun'pī	bun'pī
Bed	nan'pī	dha
Belt		
Boomerang	bŏr'an	bŏr'an
Bunya meal	na'ngū	na'ngū
Camp	kī'ra	mo'ron
Canoe	kŏm'bar (lit. bark)	
Circle	dhū	

Vocabulary

Vocabulary

ENGLISH	KABI	WAKKA
Dillie bag	ngu'am	dēm, dil'lam
Fence	wa'ra wa'ra	wa'rū wa'rū
Hat	ping'ga	
Headband		gilā'ran
House	dhu'ra	gun'dū
Knife	dhak'kē (lit. stone)	kung'gam
Nulla nulla	kū'thar	jab'ber
„ „ rectangular	bŏk'kan	
Rope	buk'kūr, yur'rū	
Shield	kun'marim, hel'-emon	gu'marī
Spear, wood	kŏn'nī	chu'iya
„ reed		ta'la ta'la
Tin vessel	kak'kar	
Tomahawk	mu'yim	mu'yīm
Water vessel		bun'dī

MISCELLANEOUS

Bark	kŏm'bar	gun'du, tan'dar, pa'ru pa'ru
Base	yauwan'nī	du'-inyī
Beauty	mun'daimun'-dainga	
Boil (tumour)	dhū'nu-ngan	dhel'an
Bottom	dhair'vī	kom'garī
Branch	kan'dīr	dyīn
Bush, the	bam'pī	bām
Camp	kī'rami, ma'rē	ma'ron
Charcoal		nguin
Claw	dhī'nang	dhī'nang
Coal	wol'ai	
Crossing-place	wang'gau wang'gau ba'ringa	yu'rumbar
Crystals, Quartz (magic)	ngan'pai, kun'dīr	nu'rūm
„ Black „ (obsidianites)	min'kŏm	

ENGLISH	KABI	WAKKA
Cut, a	dhīm	dhir'angga
Dead tree	dau'wa	dar
Doctor, native	man'ngur	wēr'nga
Dung	gu'nang	gu'nang
Edge	ka'ranī, ku'li	dain'dan
Egg	bam	ngo'a
Evil spirit	wū'bī	ma'lung
Few	bŏr'ra, dhai'ya, dhūr	
Fighting ground	bau'warī	
Flesh, *see* Meat		
Food	bin'dha	gēl
„ (tapu to minors)	mun'dha	dhir'an
Fool	nyun'dal, bŏr'raman	wān'gin
Froth	wŏr'ka	
Fur	mu'nūng	
Gammon	gut'tal	gut'āngī, ku'-tharwai
Ghost (lit. shadow)	ngu'thurū	ngul
God (the great spirit)	bī'ral	bī'ra
Half	bŏr'ra, dhang'ga, dhūr	
Half-caste	dhī-kuī	
Headman	ka'maran	
Home	yuva'thī	
Honey, native (dark bee)	gīl'la	kut'ya
„ „ (light „	ka'wai	goi'ye
Horn	bŏk'ka	
House	dhu'ra	gun'du
Inside	nŏl'lanī	
Language	bŏn'dha	gī'yam
Leader	ka'maran	
Leaves	wu'rung	
Little, a	narang'ī	
Lie (falsehood)	gut'dhal, dha'kun	
Liar	yabŏ'līman	
Log	dau'wa	dar

Vocabulary

ENGLISH	KABI	WAKKA
Lump	wul'bo	dia
Many	bŏng'gan	mai'yan
Meat	ba'ngun, mu'rang	
Messenger	dhŏm'ka	
Middle	nī'rīm, ngaran'nī	
Mourning (by fasting)	nga'rīn	
Murderer	moth'arbin	
Name	wīl	
Names of Classes	Bal'kuin	Ban'jur
„ „ „	Bar'ang	Bar'ang
„ „ „	Bŏn'da	Bŏn'da
„ „ „;	Dhĕr'wain	Chor'oin
„ „ Phratries	Dil'bai	Dil'bai or Dil'-baīin
„ „ „	Kŏp'paitthin	Kŏp'paitthin or Kŏp'paīin
Nose bubbles	bun'yu	
Noise	dil'īl	
Outside	bun'dura	
Place	dha or tya	
Red clay	kuth'ing	
River	nū'gan	kīr'ar
Road	kuan	
Root (lit. thigh)	tĕr'ang	
Sap (lit. blood)	kak'kē	
Scar (ornamental)	mū'lar	
Scrub	dhu'rī	
Seed	du'lūr	
Smell	ka	
Song	yau'war	
Sorcerer	man'ngur	wēr'nga
Spittle	nyūm	
Stink	bu'ga or bua	
Stump	kam'gīlū	
Sweat	ngu'yūm	
Taste	bŏn'dha	

ENGLISH	KABI	WAKKA
Tail	dhūn	
Tear (of the eye)	ngī'yul	ngwol
To-day	gī'lumba, ta'lī	do'rō
To-morrow	nuin'go, yīr'kī	ngu'nū ngu'nū
Top	barai'yīr, ba'rītha	
Track (and footprint)	kuan	
While, a little	tal'līya	
Wing	kun'dī	
Wood	dhū	dha'dhū
Word	bŏn'dha	gī'yam
Yesterday	ngām'ba	ngū'nē

PRONOUNS

PERSONAL

1 Sing.	I (simple)	ngai	ngi'a
„	„ (agent)	nga'dhu *or* at'yu	at'yu
„	Poss. My, Mine	ngan'yunggai	nga'ri
„	Dat. Me	ngai'bŏla	
„	Acc. Me	ngan'na	ngŏn'ya
2 Sing. Nom. (simple) Thou, You		ngin	
2 Sing. Nom.(emphatic) Thou, You		ngin'dai, ngin'bilin	
2 Sing. Nom. (agent) Thou, You		ngin'du	ngin'du
2 Sing. Poss. Thy, Thine, You, Yours		ngin'yŏnggai	ngin'gŏrī
2 Sing. Dat. Thee, You		ngin'bŏla, ngin'-bangō	
2 Sing. Acc. Thee, You		ngin'na	ngin'na
3 Sing. Nom. (simple) He, She, It		ngun'da	yoa, moa

Vocabulary

ENGLISH	KABI	WAKKA
3 Sing Nom. (agent) He, She, It	ngun'darō	
3 Sing. Poss. His, Her, Hers, Its	ngun'danō	yŏng'garī
3 Sing. Dat. Him, Her, It	ngun'dabŏla	
3 Sing. Acc. Him, Her, It	ngun'danō	mŏn"na
1 Dual Exclus. Nom. Another and I	ngŏl'ŏm	
1 and 2 Inclus. Nom. You and I	nga'līnngin	
2 Dual Inclus. Nom. You two	bu'la	
1 Plu. Nom.(simple) We	ngal'ī, ngal'īn	nga'īnga
,, ,, (agent) ,,	ngal'indō	
,, Poss. Our, Ours	ngal'īnngur, ngal'-īnnō	nga'īra
,, Dat. Us	ngal'īn-gō	
,, Acc. ,,	ngal'īn	nga'īna
2 Plu. Nom. You	ngul'am	ngū
,, Poss. Your, Yours	ngul'amō	ngūrī
,, Dat. You	ngul'ambŏla	
,, Acc.		ngū'na
,, Nom. You all	ngu'pū	
,, Poss. Yours	ngu'punū	
,, Acc. You	ngu'punga	
3 Plu. Nom. (simple) They	dhin'abū	gŏn'a
,, ,, (agent) They	dhina'buburō	
,, Poss. Their, Theirs	dhina'bunō	yau'nī
,, Dat. Them	dhina'bubŏla, dhina'-bunga	
,, Acc. ,,	dhina'bunga	yau'na

INDEFINITE

ENGLISH	KABI	WAKKA
Anyone, everyone, every-body	kar'vandhīlum	
Everyone	kŏm'kalim	

USED WITH PERSONAL PRONOUNS

Self	mit'dhī	
By oneself	mit'dhīnō	

PRONOMINAL ADJECTIVES

Another's	dhŏm'kaiyīr	
Other	kar'va	
Some . . . Others	kar'va . . . . kar'va	
This one	ka'ringa	
That one	kŏr'adhū	kŏr'ai, mŏr'a
That one's		kŏr'arī, mŏr'arī

INTERROGATIVE

Nom. (simple) Who	ngan'gai	ngan'unda
,, (agent) ,,	ngan'dō	
Poss. Whose	ngan'yunggai	
Dat. Whom	ngan'gaibŏla	
Dat. and Acc. Whom	ngā'na, ngan'gaiminī	
Nom. (simple) What	min'yanggai	nyan'da or nyan'-dī
,, (agent) ,,	ngan'dō	
,, What is the matter	wan'durŏman	wan'daran-ga

Vocabulary 241

ADJECTIVES

ENGLISH	KABI	WAKKA
Active	pī'rīkī'thum	
Afraid	wit'dhīman	bŏng'kan-ga
Alive	man'ngūr, mur'rū mīl	
	mur'rū	
Alone	mit'dhī	
Amazed	mī wu'ruwŏman	
Angry	nŏl'la bang'wŏnd-	
	amŏr'aman	
„	bang'kū, yam'ngan	
Bad	war'ang	yu'weng
Bald	nil'kan	
Big	wing'wūr	dan'dī
Black	mul'lū	nguin nguin
Blind	mī gul'ūm	ma guin
Blunt	gul'ūm	
Brave	wa wit'dhīman	wak'ka bŏng'-kan-ga
Bright	mī kak'kīman	
Brimful	tam'būrwan	tam'būr ngŏm'an
Broad	pī'ba	
Bushy	mŏt'yī	
Charmed	man'ngūr	
Cheerful	nŏl'la kala'ngūr	
Clear	ku'langūr	
Clean	kak'kal	
Clever	bun'ba	
Cold	wal'ai, walā'thau	ngyar
Cooked	ka'pī	
Cool	ya'gal	
Cowardly	wit'dhī	
Costive	dhu'ngūn dhu'pon	
Crooked	war'kun or war'kuin war'uin	

ENGLISH	KABI	WAKKA
Cruel	duma′rīman	
Curious (strange)	kar′va	
Damp	kūm′nga	
Dark	wuin′dhau	ngu-ngun
Dead	ba′luman	bwa′ngī
Deaf	pī′nang gu′lūm, ngu′rum	pē′nang guin
Dirty	mul′lū	
Done	wur′rū	
Dry	bu′thung	
Early	dhu′lura	
Easy (pace)	ngī′ta	
Empty	nŏl′la	nŏl′la
Eternal	ngam	
Every	kom′kalim	
False	dha′kūn	
Fat	brak′kē, ma′rom	
Fearful (in dread)	nŏl′la wa′rabīn	
Few	nara′ngī	
First	wur′rū	
Flat	bal′an	
Fly-blown	dingan′ga	
Full	gum′ka, wul′bung	mu′ngŏman
Foolish	nyun‘dal	
Free (gratis)	yul	
Fresh	dhu′lūr	
Frightened	wit′dhīman	bŏng′kan-ga
Giddy	mī ku′rīn, kam ku′-rīman	
Glad	nŏl′la yanggal′īn	
Good	kala′ngūr	kal′ang
Grey (of the hair)	gī′lan	
,,	dha′wudha′wul	
Greedy	yang′gan gī′vīr	
Happy	mun′dhar	

ENGLISH	KABI	WAKKA
Haughty	ngīr'bŏman	
Hard	but'dha	
Heavy	dhī'kīr	kiang'ya
High	nga'kan	
Horned	bŏk'kangur	
Hot	ma'rīman	ma'ringē
Humble	mŏ'rŏmbaluman	
Hunched	bul'tyin	
Hungry	gan'dhō	ju'roi
Ill-tempered	ku'wai gŏr'an	
Impudent	dha'bar	
Inquisitive	bī'yan	
Invincible	wup'pīn	
Itching	bī'dhaman	
Jealous	mī kam'bīman	
Kind	kŏn'anbŏman	
Lank (of animals)	dhu'ngūn gāndh'bō	
Large	wing'wur	dan'dī
Lazy	ka'wun ka'bī	
Lean	bang'undŏm dau'-wan	
Left-handed	wit'dhŏnggar	
Life-possessing, life-giving	man'ngūrngūr	
Light (in weight)	nan'dīmathī	kŏr'a kŏr'a
„ (not dark)	ngu'ruindhau	git'tē
Like (in appearance)	yī'kīman, yī'rīna	
Lively	kak'ka	
Long	gur'an	gwin'gī
Longing	nŏl'la gu'lumbŏman	
Loud	wŏp'parō, pī'naru	
Lustful	war'raiō	
Mad	pī'nang gu'lūm	
Many	bŏng'gan, gurwin'-dha	mai'yan

ENGLISH	KABI	WAKKA
More	yang'ga	
Narrow	dhal'būr	
Near-sighted	mī mu'pīman	
New	dha'līban	
Noisy	dhilīl'ngūr	
None	ka'bī	
Old	wū'rubandh *or* wū'-ruwĕndh	
One	ka'lim *or* kwa'lim	ka'buin
Other	kar'va *or* dha'ra	
Own	ngil'ka	
Overmuch	bam'guna	
Painful	kīg'yar	
Pleased	nŏl'la dhan'darban	
Pretty	mun'dai	
Quick	wai'yallo ka'lū, chuin'dō dhal'lī	
Quiet	dhī'lum, dhī'kul, kŏn'an	
Ready	ngam	
Red	bŏth'ar, ku'thingūr	kwīr
Reconciled	bu'rīmŏr'aman	
Restless	ngu'dhulā	
Right (not wrong)	yam'ba	ka'lang
Ripe	ma'rīmathī	
Rotten	bu'thī	
Scowling, supercilious	mu'rū wŏmba'līman	
Shady	bur'pū	
Sharp	mun'dū gŏr'an	
Short	dhal'būr	chung'ga
Sick	bai'yīngur	
Skinned	dhīm	
Sleepy	mī bu'wan	
Slippery, smooth	dhan'dar	
Slow	yul	ja'la

ENGLISH	KABI	WAKKA
Small	dhŏm'aramī, dha'-amī, dhŏm'mī	ka'barin
Soft	dhulū'lū	
Sorry	nŏl'la kai'yaman	
Sour	tang'kam	
Spotted	kū'nubar	
Still	dhī'kūl	
Stinking	bu'ga *or* bua *or* buga'ngūr	
Straight	dhu'rūn	ka'lang
Strong	but'dha, bau'guthar *or* bau'thar	tar'ing
Stupid	nyun'dal, bŏr'raman	
Sulky	bang'kū	
Sunny	ngui'yīm	
Surprised	nŏl'la wu'laman	
Sweet	gē'yar	ka'lang
Swollen	dhu'rumī	
Tall	gu'ran *or* gŏ'ran	gwin'gī
Tame	kŏn'an	
That	mor'anga	
Thick	wīng'wūr	
Thin	na'ran	
Thirsty	ngaiyal'lō	kung'gī
This	ka'rīnga	
Ticklish	wī'rīman	
Three	bul'la ka'lim	kor'omda
Tired	ngai'ya ba'lun	kai'ang bwa'ngē, nu'runbe
Tight	but'dha, pī'narū	
True	gī'vīr	
Two	bul'la	boi'yō
Ugly	ta'ngunba, mŏt'yī	
Unwilling	wa kai'wun nyēn'-aman	

English	Kabi	Wakka
Wall-eyed	mī wul'wīngūr	
Wanting	gu'lum	
Weak	na'man mok'kan	bu'būr
Well (in health)	man'ngūrbathin	
Wet	ding'an	
White	kak'kal	war'war
Wicked, wrong	war'ang	yu'weng
Wild	bang'gŏran, kar'um	
Willing	ka'wun nyĕn'aman	
Windy	bu'randō	
Withered	bu'thūng	

VERBS

Ache	bai'yī	
Allow	yanggalī'nŏman	
Answer	yī'kīya'man	
Awake	kin'ma	
Bathe	ku'ngū wil'lī	
Be	nyĕn'aman	ban'gē
„ born	dhak'kaman, wŏn-dŏman	
„ going to	nyanan'digō	
„ here	kadh'ī	
„ there	ngin'dī, mīn'da	
„ quiet	yul nyĕn'aman	
Beat	bai'yīman	bum'bē
Believe	gī'vīr wun'bŏmba	
Bite	kai'yathin	
Bleed (intrans.)	kak'kē baman	
Boil	ma'rīnga	
Break	kŏm'ngan, bu'rīman	kom'ngan-gē
Bring	ba'rīman	ba'ring-gē

ENGLISH	KABI	WAKKA
Buck	war'ran	
Burn (trans.)	wa'raba	
„ (intrans.)	ma'rin	
Burst	bu'lunirra	
Call	yĕl'īman	
Camp	yun'maman	yun'an
Care	ka'wun	go'woin
Carry	wŏmba'līthin	ngor'onda
Cause to drink	bīdha'līnda	
Change	ka'ringa mal'iū	
Chase	dhī'rīthin, warī'- naman	
Chew	dhin'pīman	
Chop	kang'īthin	
Climb	bŏn'yindan, wŏn'- dan	wa (imper.)
Come	ba'man, bu'gaman, ya'buai (imper.)	ba (imper.)
„ along	ya'gōbī	
„ back	bīya'bŏman	
„ down	bu'gī (imper.)	
„ here	mŏn'da	
„ „ (dog-call)	ai aiē, is is isē	ai
„ in	ka'rī ba'man	
„ out	wu'rūbŏkan, wa'bŏ- kam, gu'rūbŏkam	
„ „	bī'raman	
„ up	yu'ang (imper.)	
Converse	yathu'laiyū	
Cooey	bīyĕl'lī	
Cook		ngwau
Cover	kam'bīman, banīr'- aman	
Cross	wang'gōman	
Cry	dung'īman	
Cure	bai'yī yangga'līthin	

English	Kabi	Wakka
Cut	kau'wan, wu'lathin, wu'lam	
Delay	wŏng'galī	
Desist	wŏn'ai, wur'ū	wŏn'ya
Die	ba'luman	boi'yē
Dislike	wŏn'ai	
Dismount	nyĕn'daiō	
Distribute } Divide or deal out }	wīyu'laiyū	
Done, to be	ka'bīrŏman	
Draft	bun'gaman	
Dream	ba'rīwundaman, pa'-bunbarī	
Drink	dha'thin	dyau
Drive away	mi'bamma	
Drown (intrans.)	ka'ruman, ka'ron	
Dry	dha'līnan	
Eat	dhŏ'man, dhau	dya
Enter	ka'rīthin, ka'rimī	
Exchange	wīyu'laiyū	wung'jau
Fall	bumba'līn	yir'angē
„ upon	wŏmba'līman	
Feel	bŏn'dhŏman	
Fetch	ba'rīman	ba'ring-gē
Fight	baiyu'laiyū	bum'jau
Find	ba'tyīman	
Fly (as birds)	dhu'raman	
Forget	pī'nang ba'luman, ngara'lŏman	
Forgive	bŏn'na kŏn'an wŏn'-imba	
Gape	wul'lai	
Get on	ba'tyimī	
Give	wum'ngan, wuga (imper.)	wām'ga, wī'ya
Gnaw	dhan'dhŏman	

Vocabulary

ENGLISH	KABI	WAKKA
Go	yan'man, yan'gō	yan'gō
„ home	yan'mare	
„ in	kar'imī	
„ under	kor'imgai	
Grasp	kŏl'bathin	
Grow	dhū'ruman	dī'ya
Haste	ngam (imper.)	
Hate	wa ka'wun	wak'ka go'woin
Have	kai'mīn'da	-gan (enclitic)
Hear	brŏng'aman, vrŏng'- aman	bi'yanga
Help	ngu'pŏnathin	
Hit	bun'baman	bum'bē
Issue	bī'raman	
Joke	dha'rīthin	
Jump	yau'warra, war'rai	
Kick	na'ruman	
Kill	baī'yiman	bum'jinga
Kiss	dham'būr bun'bithin	
Know	vrŏng'aman, brŏng'- aman	bi'yanga
Laugh	wa'thīman	
Leave	wŏn'aimathī, yīva'- rī	
„ (abandon)	wŏn'damathī	
Lend	timba'rowa	
Let (allow)	wum'ngan (lit. give)	
„ go	bīn'dha	
„ out	wu'rūwathin	
Lie (speak falsely)	yabŏl'īman, dha'- kun ya	
„ (recline)	yun'maman	yun'auwa
Lift	bun'ma	wa'yima
Light (kindle)	ba'raiyō	
„ (alight)	ngan'dabŏman	

P

ENGLISH	KABI	WAKKA
Like	ka'wun	go'woin
Live	mu'rūnyĕn'aman, mu'rūbaman	mīl ngyin'anga
Look	nai'yīlathin, na'kan	
Lose	ngara'loman	
Love	balū'raman	
Make	yang'gōman	yang'ga
Make cry	dunginū'raman	
Mark	bandh'ngūr	
Marry	bin'dhamathī, dhŏm'ŏman	bin'da
Mend	yīl'vanya, bau'waman	
Mount	wŏng'alī	
Obey	kā'lū vrŏng'aman	
Perambulate	wak'karin yan'diriū	
Play	bīwa'thin	
Prepare	nau'wapīra	
Pull	yu'rī	
Put	yīva'rī	
,, away	mīva'rī	
,, in	karī'naman, mō'aman	
,, out	wuru yīva'rīthinī	
,, up	wŏmba'thin	
Relish	nōl'la bau'wan	
Remain	nyĕn'am, yīn'mai	
Remember	pī'nang bama'thī	pī'nangba
Resemble	yī'kīman	
Return	bīya'bŏman, bīyam'-gaiyō, bŏm'kŏman	
Revolve	ku'rīman	
Ride	kang'kīthin	
Rise	wŏn'dŏman	
Roast	kī'raba mŏr'ba	
Roll	dhinda'līman	
Run	bidha'līthin	jia
Scold	yam'nguman	

ENGLISH	KABI	WAKKA
Scratch	dhū′ma	
Search	kauwa′liū, wa′karraiō, wŏr′raman	
See	nŏm′ngathī	nā′ngī
Seek	nar′riū	
Send	bīn′dha	
Separate	ban′yau	
Shake	dhu′wa	
Shell	mī′bīra	
Shoot	bun′bara	
Show	ngŏm′ba	
Sing	dŏp′pathin, yau′ar dŏp′pa	yau′arkun′dama
Sink	nyin′daman	
Sit	nyĕn′aman	ngyin′au
Skin	nŏl′la wul′la	
Sleep	buan′dō yun′maman	buan′dō yun′auwa
Smash	bŏn′dhīra	
Smell	ba′līman	
Smoke (a pipe)	pai′yum kai′yathin (or kai′yaman)	
Speak	ya′man	ya′yau
„ quickly	yĕlyĕl′īman	
Spear	bau′wa	
Split	wul′la	
Spring up	yī′raman	
Squeeze	bulunīr′aman, nau′waman	
„	ngu′nīra, wŏr′a bu′dhaman	
Stand	bu′bai, buwan	ban′gē
Steal	kŏr′raman	
Sting	bau′waman	
Stop (arrest)	kakka′riū	
„ (remain)	nyĕn′aman	
Strengthen, hold fast	bu′dhawathin	

ENGLISH	KABI	WAKKA
Strike	bai'yīman	bum'bē
Struck, to get	ngŏn'dai	
Suck	bun'bīthin	
Sweat	ngū'yūmbŏman	
Swell	dhu'rumī	dī'ya
Swim	yungga'thin	
Take	bunma'lī, kang'gō, kŏm'-ngan	bī
„ back	bīya'vindiū	
„ in (admit)	karīn'dimī	
Taste	yavan'dha	
Teach	ngutana'liū	
Tell	ya'man	ya
Tell a lie	dha'kun ya	nyu'labai
Think	vrŏng'aman	bi'yanga
Throng	kaka'rīman	
Throw	ting'gathin	
„ (down)	bŏmka'numan	
Tire (trans.)	ngai'ya ba'luna	
Try	nga'tanī, wu'tyangalī	
Turn (intrans.)	ku'rīgō	
„ (trans.)	kurī'naman	
Unable, to be	ka'bī	
Wait	wŏn'mīman	
Walk	yul yan'man	yan'andē
Want (require)	wandha'rŏman	
Warm	wa'kōbŏra	
Wash	kak'kal yiva'rī	
Watch	nyinan'dīman	
Weep	du'ngīman	du'nga
Whisper	wŏp'pa yĕl'lī	
Whistle	kuī'bī	
Wipe	kak'kal gīra'ngilīthin	
Work	yuang'biniliū	
Wring the neck	kun'namara	

ADVERBS

INTERROGATIVE

ENGLISH	KABI	WAKKA
How	min'yanggō	win'yuramau, wan'darumau
How getting on	wen'yarī	
How is it	wan'dyuramathī	wan'daraiyu
How many	min'yama	nyam'ma
Whatever	wen'yiragō	
What place	minya'nū	
When	wen'yō	wen'yuala
When (at what time)	wen'yobŏla	wen'yowŏla
Where	wen'ya	wen'yu
Wherever	wen'yominī	wen'yamga
,,	wen'yiragō	
Which way	wan'yiram	
Whither	ngan'gaibŏla	
Why	wan'dhurathin, mina'nī, mina'lō	nan'go

GENERAL

Above	bar'itha	
After, behind	bī'ya, bīya'nī	bī'yān
Afterwards	bŏn'a gī'ra	
Almost	bar	
Alone	kā'lim	
Also	yī'kī	
Always	ngam	
Back	bī'ya, bŏk'a	
,,		bu'rumia
Badly	war'ang	yu'weng
Before	wu'rūnī	
By and by	bŏn'na wŏp'pa	

ENGLISH	KABI	WAKKA
Close	nŏl'la	
Directly (at once)	dha'lī	
Early	dha'li, dhu'lura	
Eternally	ngam	
Everywhere	kŏ'la nga kŏ'la, wen'-yō nga wen'yō	
Far	mu'kīr	
Farther	kila'thunda	
Fast	kā'lŭ	
Firmly	but'dha, pī'narū	
First	wu'rū	
For	ka'rī	
Gently	wŏp'pa	
Good (very well)	a'thī	
Go on (try)	ya	
Head first	kam'iyan	
Headwards(by the head)	kam'ngūr	
Here	ka'rī, kar'īnda, ka'-thī, kaī	kai, -gan
If	bŏn'a, wen'yō	
Just now	kai	
Late	ngam	
Likewise	yī'kī	
More	yang'ga	
Near	pīra'nī	
Never	wa	
No	ka'bī, wa, wak'ka	wak'ka
Noisily	dhilīl'bangūr	
Not	ka'bī, wa	
„ (imperatively)	bar, wa'gō	wak'ka
Nowhere	ka'bī	
Often	kir'wa, ngam	
On foot	dhī'nang-gō	
On horseback	nan'ngur	
Other side	gun'manī	mar'ang-ginī
Out	wu'rū	

Vocabulary

ENGLISH	KABI	WAKKA
Perhaps, probably	ĭm′ba	yām′ga
Really	ngin′dī	
Slowly	wŏp′pa, yul	
That side	nyŏn′da nyŏn′danī	
„	kŏl′a dhu′rūnī	
That way	nga′lŏma	
There	kŏl′a, mŏt′ya	
This place	mŏn′da	
This side	bar′inga, ka′rīdhu′- rūnī	kar′ang-ginī
This way	yĕr′rī	yē′ama
Thus	yīrī, yī′rīn	
Top	bar′īnga, bar′ītha	
Under	tar′vanō	
Vainly, in vain, for nothing	yul	
Very, very much	kar′va	
Well, rightly	yam′bō	
Whether or not	wen′yamba	
While	bŏn′a	
Yes	yauai, yo	ya
Yonder	mŏr′amai	

CONJUNCTIONS

Also	yī′kī	
And	nga	gŏn′a
If	bŏn′a, wen′yō	
When	„ „	wen′yowol′a
While	bŏn′a	

INTERJECTIONS

Alas	wai	
All right	yau′a yau′ai	

ENGLISH	KABI	WAKKA
Ay, here I am	o'	
By no means	wa wa	
Dear dear	a-rī-rŏm	
Go on, try	ya	
Good	ath'ī	
Halloo, hi	a'rau, nga'ra	
Indeed	ī'nga	
Just so, so	ē'yīla, ī'la, yau'-aimba	
Very well	e'	
Well	a'	
Well done	kala'ngūr, ka'burau	
Wonderful	gin'dī, a-rī-rŏm	
Signifying—		
Anger	m	
Pleasure	a-rī-rŏm	
Possibility, uncertainty	im'ba	
Regret	ē	
Self-satisfaction	moun	
Surprise	gin'dī, go-gin'dī	

PARTICLES

Belonging to	-man	-man'na
Causation, concurrence	-a'ngī	
Motion	-gō	-gō
Possession	-ka'rī	-gu'ra, -man
Presence		-gŏn

For EU product safety concerns, contact us at Calle de José Abascal, 56–1°,
28003 Madrid, Spain or eugpsr@cambridge.org.

www.ingramcontent.com/pod-product-compliance
Ingram Content Group UK Ltd.
Pitfield, Milton Keynes, MK11 3LW, UK
UKHW010344140625
459647UK00010B/808